Psychoanalysis: A Very Short Introduction

VERY SHORT INTRODUCTIONS are for anyone wanting a stimulating and accessible way into a new subject. They are written by experts, and have been translated into more than 45 different languages.

The series began in 1995, and now covers a wide variety of topics in every discipline. The VSI library now contains over 500 volumes—a Very Short Introduction to everything from Psychology and Philosophy of Science to American History and Relativity—and continues to grow in every subject area.

Titles in the series include the following:

Daniel Pick

PSYCHOANALYSIS

A Very Short Introduction

OXFORD
UNIVERSITY PRESS

OXFORD
UNIVERSITY PRESS

Great Clarendon Street, Oxford, OX2 6DP,
United Kingdom

Oxford University Press is a department of the University of Oxford.
It furthers the University's objective of excellence in research, scholarship,
and education by publishing worldwide. Oxford is a registered trade mark of
Oxford University Press in the UK and in certain other countries

© Daniel Pick 2015

The moral rights of the author have been asserted

First edition published in 2015

Published in the United States of America by Oxford University Press
198 Madison Avenue, New York, NY 10016, United States of America

British Library Cataloguing in Publication Data
Data available

Library of Congress Control Number: 2014959011

ISBN 978-0-19-922681-8

Printed and bound by
CPI Group (UK) Ltd, Croydon, CR0 4YY

To Anna and Tasha

Contents

Acknowledgements

I have benefitted from conversations about this subject with more colleagues, friends, and members of my family than I can acknowledge here. But I want to mention at least a few debts of gratitude. For generously responding to drafts, warning of pitfalls and/or discussing the essential ingredients of a very short introduction to psychoanalysis, my warm thanks to Isobel Pick, Irma Brenman Pick, the late Eric Brenman, David Bell, Michael Brearley, Don Campbell, Elizabeth Coates-Thümmel, Josh Cohen, Penny Driver, Matt ffytche, Stephen Frosh, Keith Jacobs, Jonathan Lear, Matthew Reisz, Lyndal Roper, Jacqueline Rose, Priscilla Roth, and John Steiner. I am also indebted to Nicole Mennell for some background research, Dan Harding for copy editing, Matias Lopez-Portillo, Dan Hind, and Andrea Keegan for editorial comments, and the anonymous OUP reader for a number of additional helpful suggestions.

Chapter 1
Introduction

Two people, a patient and psychoanalyst, meet at set times each week; the patient is free to say whatever comes to mind. Sometimes the psychoanalyst might act as catalyst, speaking in order to help the patient who is silent and blocked; or might also clarify, underline something striking, and then interpret what has been said or done. Interpretation here means to draw out latent meanings. The patient perhaps agrees or disagrees, moves off at a tangent, adding detail, feeling moved and well understood, or positively annoyed. He or she makes use of an interpretation or not. They talk and listen to each other, or sometimes fail to. Through these encounters, an unusual opportunity exists to explore the workings of the patient's mind, and to bring about change.

Psychoanalysis was first used for adults, then later also adapted to work with children. Its profound impact is well illustrated in case studies produced by the founder of this tradition, Sigmund Freud (1856–1939) and in numerous reports by his followers. Freud's daughter, Anna, herself an analyst, described in 1929 her treatment of an eleven-year-old boy with a confused sexual identity, who oscillated between aggressive behaviour, violent remorse, depression, and fixed beliefs, such as the need to touch a knob on the wall of the WC three times and immediately afterwards to do the same to a knob on the other side. She uncovered how he had identified himself with a god 'sitting on a great throne in the courts of Heaven', with knobs to left and right. 'If he pressed a knob on one side, some human being died: if he pressed one on the other side a child was born into the world.' Psychoanalysis, she showed, may help a person be less driven by such omnipotent beliefs and enslaving compulsions. Soon after, an English colleague, Ella Sharpe, lectured her students on the positive difference that this form of treatment made to a young woman overwhelmed by anxiety attacks and temper tantrums, another who arrived in a state of utter dejection, and a third, an obsessional man, who lived in terror of his powerful impulses to jump out of the window.

A detailed description of psychoanalysis is to be found in the story of Richard, a gifted, unhappy, and frequently terrified ten-year-old, who saw Melanie Klein for four months during World War II. From the age of eight Richard was so unwell he could not attend school; he was frightened of other children, prey to frequent illnesses, given over to cruel impulses, and prone to severely depressed moods. The terrifying conflict raging in the world outside was a factor, but far from the only one, fuelling Richard's inhibitions, hypochondria, and loneliness. In a remarkable book, Klein detailed the things Richard said in each session, and the drawings he produced, conveying the manner in which she sought, as an analyst, to understand his anxiety, feelings of hate, fear of being hated, and desperate neediness. Even though she regarded the treatment as incomplete when terminated, Klein reported the significant changes that occurred in Richard: he recovered a capacity to learn, and was more secure and trusting of those upon whom he depended. Her account suggested how Richard became more loving, and more confident that he was loved; he was less caught up with his own destructive fantasies, enjoyed stronger relationships with his parents, expressed greater hopefulness about his future, and seemed far better equipped to thrive.

Psychoanalysis (or for brevity's sake just 'analysis') is both a strikingly original method of therapy and a distinct body of knowledge about which strong claims have been made, for and against. It is hard to classify, as it does not fit smoothly into pre-existing categories of science, social science, historical methodology, philosophy, literature, or art. This approach has always drawn upon cultural ideas of the time, but Freud also brought into being something distinctly new. In this book, I focus especially upon the *clinical attitude* that Freud created and the reason why it might facilitate important psychic change. My aim is to tell a story of present-day practice, while tracing various roots in the past. Since analysts have never stopped revering and drawing upon Freud, while also often arguing with or developing his ideas, he remains a crucial foundation for the contemporary story.

Freud sought to create a new kind of laboratory and clinic rolled into one: the analytic consulting room. No technical equipment is needed for this procedure and no medication prescribed; the only essential furniture is chairs and a couch, although for children a few basic toys that can be put to multiple uses are also provided, along with paper, pencils, paint, etc. Analysis is not as straightforward, however, as this stark description suggests, and clinicians still grapple with the difficulty of practising this endlessly fascinating craft.

Analysis then is an approach to mind, its creative functioning and its many afflictions. Countless patients have made use of it, one way or another. Many but by no means all have claimed to find it beneficial; some feel they would not have survived without it.

Freud first used the term 'psychoanalysis' in 1896. In modern parlance, psyche tends to mean simply mind, but the word still echoes faintly the original Greek sense of soul, or even breath of life; the 'analysis' part of Freud's phrase implies the examination and differentiation of the particular elements that make up a structure. The movement that Freud founded has a complex history. He set many hares running, revisited and then challenged his own formulations, and wrote so prolifically that his works occupy over twenty volumes in the landmark set of English translations known as *The Standard Edition*. Although not all his ideas neatly cohere, there are common threads. Above all, analysts still share Freud's guiding theory that thoughts can exist in our minds of which we are unconscious. True, many writers had represented the unconscious before; but Freud stressed the *dynamic* process involved: we actively shut things out from awareness or distort thoughts we cannot tolerate. And these jarring, discarded mental contents may then lodge as unconscious aspects of our own minds, or sometimes return to trouble conscious awareness afresh.

The analyst is tasked with attending to possible unconscious meaning in what the patient brings. But analysis can equally be seen as an art—for the practitioner—of self-restraint. It requires effort to forgo the conventions of ordinary conversational exchange, thereby to provide this different opportunity for communication. Admittedly, divergent schools of thought regarding both theory and practice have evolved. Even so, most analysts would aim to hold themselves back, trying not to provide conventional 'prompts', nor set the agenda, nor again to be conventionally reassuring. Indeed, the analyst tries not to take for granted what the other 'must' really mean, but rather allows ample room for the patient to speak (or in the case of children to play) at will, and see where thoughts lead. Analysis can provide a rare space in which a complex life story or the most fleeting thoughts of the moment are listened to without constraint or moralistic criticism, and in which ultimately it is the patient who has the opportunity to encounter features of his or her own mind, previously unavailable to their consciousness.

In an autobiographical study published in 1925, Freud described the method he had developed—*free association*—to facilitate access to the unconscious. In his pre-analytic days, he had asked patients to concentrate on particular subjects. Part of his genius was to be able to shift gear when prompted, in fact, by patients who *wanted* him to listen to what they were saying. The point was not for the doctor to dictate, nor simply diagnose, but, crucially, to let the patient talk at will. So Freud would routinely encourage his patient at the outset of treatment 'to say whatever comes into his head, while ceasing to give any conscious direction to his thoughts'.

Freud advised his patients to try to disregard nothing, however painful, humiliating, or apparently meaningless. Such 'demand for candour', he added, is 'the precondition of the whole analytic treatment'. Its purpose is to gain access to otherwise 'repressed material'. In polite conversation, there is much it is imprudent or indelicate to say. But even invited to speak freely, the patient may also 'resist' without meaning to, and this can be evident in stumbling over words, drawing to a halt, or losing track, when thoughts generate conflict and anxiety. In fact, nobody can simply 'free associate' on demand. People discard their own ideas as 'unimportant', when in reality they may be too discomforting to broach. It becomes clear how much trouble we have tolerating certain phenomena in the privacy of our own minds, let alone when another is present.

For analysts, the patient's meanings are to be discovered, not assumed in advance, so if a person arrives and says, 'I hate Christmas', 'do you take cash?', or 'I saw a black cat as I entered your front garden', we know the literal meaning, but it is an open question what such statements really signify, and why they are uttered now. The analyst tries to interest the patient in that open question of meaning, and to listen with composure to whatever is brought up. Where resistance is light, the practitioner interprets what is revealed of the unconscious content. The patient's speech, analysis proposes, can afford glimpses of ideas or fantasies beyond the subject's control. Where resistance is strong (for example the patient falls silent, or becomes angry when a troubling matter is approached) the analyst focuses upon that defensiveness, recognizing its character, 'and will explain it to the patient'. Freud was more didactic than later clinicians might consider appropriate, but his point remains central: the analyst pays heed to what is expressed, while exploring how the patient may have opted (often quite unwittingly) to avoid seeing or knowing. Freud did not mean just that we are unable to recall everything at once; rather, he argued that we often remove from our consciousness what excites and/or troubles us even while we may be unaware that this is what we have done.

Freud made a studied effort to analyse himself; he sought candidly to record puzzling behaviour, dreams, and perturbing thoughts. Despite his scientific background and commitment to reason, he found evidence of unexpected, negative feelings towards loved ones, a minefield of anxieties, possessive wishes regarding his mother, hostile attitudes towards his father and sons, superstitious dread of his own early death, and strange moments when he would forget or confuse the most crucial things. Even particular words, he showed, might suddenly and completely elude a person, because of their uncomfortable, unconscious meanings.

Friends and patients played their part in his searching inquiries; Freud seemed to need, throughout, someone to argue with, as well as trusted colleagues with whom he could bounce ideas around. His correspondence was voluminous. Freud is sometimes cast (or cast himself) as a solitary figure, but he also saw how interdependent people are, whatever protestations they may make about being alone, or self-made; he concluded in a study, *Group Psychology*, that

> In the individual's mental life someone else is invariably involved, as a model, as an object, as a helper, as an opponent; and so from the very first individual psychology, in this extended but entirely justifiable sense of the words, is at the same time social psychology.

Freud also realized that analysis creates a highly charged emotional situation; it is a social interaction that is shadowed, and sometimes entirely over-run, by powerful unconscious attitudes. Initially he found the volatile dynamics surprising, but his work would show again and again why and how these passions flared up in treatment. An individual's attitude to the analyst, he noted, taps into unconscious feelings, and moves between a positive and negative character, from 'the extremes of a passionate, completely sensual love' to 'the unbridled expression of an embittered defiance and hatred'. It is in the nature of mind, he believed, to transfer on to new situations, albeit often entirely unconsciously, earlier thoughts, scenes, or relationships, most of which stem ultimately from infancy. In analysis, patients may gain insight into these tendencies, and thereafter be less inclined to repeat patterns blindly and in perpetuity.

Being a patient or an analyst affects people differently, but it is likely to be vexed; an emotionally raw and difficult, not merely intellectual, experience for both. It troubles its participants in more ways than one. Analysts try to maintain an even keel, but it is now considered a crucial part of their role to be open to the patient's unconscious communication and to make use of the way they are affected by it in order to interpret. People can become agitated by analysis, and in turn have an impact on their analysts, who may at times find themselves more depressed, excited, restless, angry, listless, sluggish, anxious, dreamy, or whatever else, than they felt before the session. It can also be an engrossing, exhilarating, and moving experience for both.

Freud offered the ideal of an analyst imperturbably listening, without complying or running away. But some followers considered more fully how both patient and practitioner, like any other couple or larger but still intimate group, are unconsciously affected by each other, and how this awareness can be used to explore what some analysts refer to as 'the inner world'. The analytic model presupposes that much communication passes below our conscious radar, or entirely outside formal language, and that aspects of our minds will always inevitably remain obscure. Yet Freud's approach is also appropriately described as a *talking* cure, a means of putting hitherto unspeakable and unknown things back into discourse, for a therapeutic purpose.

An emergency call

Freud and other major pioneers offered important advice on technique. But practitioners (novice or otherwise) inevitably experience unforeseen dilemmas. Consider a disturbed man, Rob, who burst into his session, soon after beginning treatment with his analyst, panic stricken. 'Quick, an emergency, as I was walking here...a crazy woman...baby being hurt...must call police at once; please pass your phone.' The analyst faced a predicament: was the danger outside real, requiring that he agreed to the request? He was under intense pressure to act, but managed to propose instead of instantly dialling the emergency services that they talk about it first.

Thereupon Rob, mildly relieved, sat down and said, more slowly, that he had witnessed a mother wheeling a pram; he was *almost* sure that there was something wrong; he *suspected* she was reaching into her bag for a weapon, and had had the thought (triggered when she pulled out cigarettes) that she intended harm, even to set the blanket on fire. He recalled the baby screaming just when she reached down and he then feared violence was imminent, and panicked. As he spoke, the feeling of alarm lessened and 'facts' blurred. He muttered, 'maybe I over-reacted... I'm not sure what happened'. In this case the phone call was not required. Eventually the analyst learned more of Rob's early circumstances and exposure to danger, as a baby and toddler, when his mother had taken drugs. The street scene crisis that had seemed so real started to take on features more akin to a dream.

At this early stage Rob idealized treatment and said he had the highest opinion of his analyst. He was soon to take a different view, with alternating rage, panic, and threats. He felt inflamed by the therapeutic situation he was in, and also stoked things up. Occasionally it proved possible to make interpretations, and for Rob to regard these as tolerable, even perhaps useful for a bit. But the sessions stirred him up more and more, making him unmanageably excited; Rob stopped attending some months after, and the analyst never saw him again.

Aims

Sometimes analysis succeeds impressively in helping a person change, as could be seen with Richard, or proves difficult, and may end precipitately, or without yielding much benefit, as was perhaps the case with Rob. The outcome might well depend on the patient's attitude and condition, the technique, experience, and qualities of the analyst, and a hard-to-define 'chemistry' that takes place between them. The analyst attempts to maintain a particular stance and, where possible, to address a person's conflicts. And yet this inquiry can stir up a patient's profound opposition. Rob said on one occasion that he craved firm guidance, wanted his analyst to 'take his side' against certain enemies, and regarded interpretations as mostly useless. Patients probably all feel that at one time or another; some, however, tolerate the frustration of being enjoined to think about things more easily than others: the analyst seeks to provide interpretations, although patients may demand advice, a call to action, or instant agreement.

Psychoanalysis endeavours to bring about change, but it is not some miracle remedy. When it is successful, patients are better able to make use of their minds for thinking, and know more of their own passions. It might assist a person to feel less helpless, see new perspectives on a given situation, be more spontaneous, and have greater internal forbearance. It aims to enable patients to face their limitations and conflicts, but also find greater strength to know and bear who they are. Its advocates suggest it

9

can help us achieve a greater integration, but in the recognition that it is always a fantasy to imagine being entirely at one with ourselves. Freud suggested we are always psychically divided, fractured within, and to some extent strangers to ourselves. Yet analysis may enable a patient to put together more pieces in their jigsaws, stand having feelings previously not tolerated, bear more guilt without becoming utterly crushed by it, cope better with anxiety, and forgo a need to inflict it immediately upon others.

Analysis has also provided countless illustrations of how particular (but of course not all) bodily symptoms may derive from a person's unconscious feelings and conflicts. Freud suggested on one occasion how a hysterical patient 'absent-mindedly' staged a particular scene, in gestures, even while cancelling it out: one hand busy unbuttoning their own clothes, as the other quickly refastened them. Yet this person was not consciously thinking of sexual desire, nor aware at that point of anxiety or counter-thoughts in her mind. The body can tell a story, and sometimes this can then be made explicit in words. It is often the case in an analysis that particular physical 'complaints' recede, as the process goes on.

For some, psychoanalysis proves a grimmer task than for others, but none of us can do such work without discomfort and sadness, nor fully alone. This is not to say that treatment delivers benefits to all. And although analysis makes some general claims it is not a fixed philosophy, nor is it a bundle of rules or principles that the patient learns. Of course, like most things it can be mystified or treated as a dogma. But when revered and rigidified in such ways, Freud's insistently experimental approach, provisional findings, and inventive style are all too easily lost.

Analysts have yardsticks for good outcomes: an enhanced capacity to endure ordinary everyday unhappiness rather than succumb to hysterical misery (as Freud once remarked); an ability to love and work; become more able to play, think, and dream; tolerate doubt; regard ourselves and others in less split fashion (e.g. where we perceive a loved one as pure, only to project bad, unwanted qualities into someone or something else); view our contradictions with greater irony; be less in thrall to harsh, unconscious self-reproaches; or face up to the enigma and endlessness of our own desires. As the analyst Jacques Lacan showed, it is an illusion to imagine desire is akin to need: a thirsty person's demand for water can be met, whereas the desire, say, for love or reassurance may know no bounds.

However, in good practice such aims would not be pushed at patients: to do so would undermine the analytic approach. Patients bring stories and fields of concern; the analyst then responds specifically to what is brought, trying to contain and respond to the other's communications, periodically venturing interpretations (those attempts to address the underlying situation, and also to foster the patient's own further thoughts and associations), in the hope that these interventions are useful, and if not, to explore why they fail to be so.

Analysts have often written about how patients, even while devoutly wishing for change, and paying for treatment, may unconsciously opt, even fiercely, to keep the status quo. There can even be what is called a 'negative therapeutic reaction' when things appear to go well in treatment, perhaps because feeling better might evoke a sense of guilt, or even the patient's fear of disloyalty to the 'ill' part of themselves. We may also feel a powerful need to leave aspects of our minds lodged in a psychosomatic condition, or in another person (someone who is meant to carry our unwanted feelings or ideas), a fog of malaise, or fixed convictions about the way the world is. It is, after all, common knowledge that people at times wish to blot things out, anaesthetize themselves with work, drink, drugs, or a computer screen, and insist nothing is wrong, or that the other is entirely at fault. Whatever factors, internal and external, might drive someone to seek treatment, they can still subsequently feel ambivalent towards it, not least because even the most neurotic states of mind may have a self-protective function: a person might use one set of symptoms, for example obsessional habits, to guard against others, such as paranoid dreads, that are intuited to be worse.

Who is treatment for?

Patients can find entering analysis frightening *and* emancipating; to be allowed to have moods without being fussed over or expected to 'get over it' might be helpful; even, for some, a new and liberating experience. It may also be an extraordinary relief to be in touch with the depressed, and even madder, parts of oneself. However, for those on the edge of or in the midst of psychosis, or thinly defended against death wishes, the analytic approach may prove especially difficult, risking a renewed breakdown when the analyst cannot provide a longed-for permanent refuge. Some find the treatment stirs up overwhelming anxieties, and the pattern of intense involvement followed by sudden separations, such as weekends or holidays, may just be too difficult to bear. An assessment of *capacity for analysis* thus has to take place beforehand and be held in mind by the therapist during treatment.

Opinion divides on whether analysis *can* be made suitable for patients in psychotic states, and if so how. These states admittedly take many forms: they can be transient or chronic, so it depends also on what type and with what severity. But when a person is hallucinating, or otherwise seriously deluded, they may see the analyst or her interpretations entirely according to their darkest or most manic fantasy, and might register a comment, for instance 'you suspect I have evil intentions towards you', or, 'you long to live with me here', as indubitably confirming the validity of the very thing they fear or desire. All patients can experience interpretations as if they were legal verdicts or moral judgements (a world of 'ought' and 'ought not') delivered from 'on high', but for some this can have an absolutely inflexible quality.

To say someone is in a psychotic state is not to say they are beyond all comprehension. Freud was part of a venerable tradition in his close explorations of the meanings and experience of madness. He produced a penetrating study of the psychic predicaments of the one-time judge, Daniel Paul Schreber, who had penned a remarkable report, *Memoirs of My Nervous Illness*. Schreber believed his nerves to be in contact with cosmic rays, and that he was required to fulfil a mission to redeem the world and restore it to its former state of blessedness. This was to be achieved by his being transformed into a woman so that he could have intercourse with God and so save the world. Freud's report (based on the patient's text, not analytic treatment) made a major contribution to understanding psychosis. Among his insights was the recognition that a delusional belief may be an attempted 'patch' to restore some semblance of meaning and structure, after the illness has shattered it.

For Freud, no patient, psychotic or neurotic, is *merely* 'babbling': the particular symptoms, however strange, may in fact be a person's desperate means to recover from psychic chaos. Despite acknowledging method in madness, Freud doubted the applicability of his treatment directly to the psychotic. Some of his early followers, such as Sándor Ferenczi, were more hopeful on this score, and extended treatment to those so ill that more cautious colleagues rejected them. He was said to be the master of difficult cases. After World War II, more experimentation with analysis for psychotic patients followed. In England, Hanna Segal, Wilfred Bion, and Herbert Rosenfeld, for example, analysed patients who had very serious long-term mental health problems. Even with people diagnosed with schizophrenia, they stuck as best they could to making interpretations, inspired by Klein and her bold clinical work with children.

Such analytic encounters produced some interesting and moving results, sometimes getting through and offering emotional containment, albeit in the gravest cases affording little prospect of cure. A remarkable American law professor, Elyn Saks, hospitalized in Oxford and at Yale during her studies, diagnosed with depression, and then full-blown schizophrenia, suggests what can be achieved through a combination, in her case, of psychoanalytic work, medication, extremely loyal friends and, later, a partner, even in the direst psychological conditions. But her book also graphically shows the risks and dangers analytic treatment holds for a patient at the mercy of delusional thoughts, as when she refuses to leave the premises, or arrives at a session armed with a knife.

Many people now complain that the ever more prolific medications on offer from psychiatrists lead to numbing of the mind; evidence exists about the overblown claims previously made by pharmaceutical companies, and the damaging side-effects that many of the drugs in the medical arsenal can cause. Some do indeed find prescribed drugs helpful, even life saving, in alleviating terror, delusions, or suicidal despair. And in certain instances, as with Saks, analytic treatments take place while patients are also receiving medication. Analysts may or may not be psychiatrists themselves. But in analytical work, they, like most patients, would assume it preferable, wherever possible, to conduct therapy without the requirement for a person artificially to subdue or alter their own mental states in this way.

How best, if at all, to conduct psychoanalysis with psychotic patients has been much discussed. Certainly most analysts would argue that the approach may have to be modified to some extent in light of a patient's serious mental illness: i.e. when, as Saks puts it, 'the wall that separates fantasy from reality dissolves'. The aim, say with a schizophrenic patient, might be for the delusions to lose some of their intensity, even in the knowledge that they may never fully and permanently disappear. However, a modification in the power of a person's psychotic 'voices', for example, could itself be of great benefit; indeed, the patient may at times find it valuable simply to have somebody consistently struggling to hear them and search for their meanings. Analytic work with psychotic patients has also helped us know more about extreme pathological states and the more disturbed, even psychotic, aspects of the ordinarily neurotic person.

The Canadian historian Barbara Taylor, long a resident of Britain, has, like Saks, made a strong case for the talking cure, in her case during a severe and prolonged depression. In a recent book, she unflinchingly charts her descent, years of alcohol, pills, ever worse self-hatred and harm, and then relates her impressive recovery, assisted by her long-standing analyst 'V', a network of close friends, a far-seeing psychiatrist, not to mention the sheltering, if decaying, hospital, the 'brick mother', in which she found her asylum. Taylor recognizes her opportunity to receive hospital care *and* continue throughout with intensive analysis is all too rare, both for economic reasons, and because many psychiatrists frown upon Freud's methodology. She also shows how an old system of hospital-based treatment in Britain, while riddled with problems, was for many a life-saving refuge. She charts the deteriorating, sometimes dreadful conditions former inmates have faced since the closure of the large asylums in the last quarter of the 20th century. This influential policy (driven by a range of factors, including the pressure to cut costs and a critique of 'total institutions') was followed by all too little of the promised alternative of community-based care.

Yet, we may ask, what has drawn people who would not meet psychiatric definitions of mental illness to undertake analysis? Why bother? This book examines why one might choose such a substantial commitment—not only in a state of desperation and breakdown, but also in search of personal development, insight, and creativity.

Patients might come with a problem in mind, perhaps a mysterious unexplained illness or unforeseen life crisis. Some turn to analysis when a pattern of behaviour and belief is no longer working to hold things together, or when they intuit that some psychological factor is sabotaging their own better interests.

Perhaps changed circumstances—such as a new job, a marriage, a child, divorce, or bereavement—throws everything into confusion. A person might seek treatment complaining of a puzzling physical symptom, something painfully missing, a phobia, uncontainable anxiety, or existence under a 'black sun' (Julia Kristeva's title for her eloquent study of melancholia). Motives are not only overt; they are to be discovered rather than assumed in advance, whatever the preliminary, 'official' problem.

In medical practice a patient can present rather passively for examination, then follow prescribed treatments; if all goes to plan, the person gets better. In analysis, however, you cannot bypass the experience and 'cut to the chase'; what is therapeutic is not the imposition of a solution but the continuing work carried out over time. In the classical approach in Britain, the patient attends five times weekly; three times a week is standard in France. There are such noticeable differences between analytic subcultures, although in fact many analysts accept patients for less frequent sessions too. Analysis is not pain free, nor is it instant. On the other hand, it may also prove enjoyable, funny, and more carefree too. Certainly, a sense of psychological labour, of something demanding *and* potentially creative, looms large in analytic vocabulary. 'Work' of various kinds, Freud suggested, occurs both consciously and unconsciously: he spoke of 'dream work', 'the work of mourning', 'working through'.

Analysis, or...?

Even if we recognize our neuroses or 'mind-forg'd manacles' as disabling, we may not be able to loosen their grip through our own efforts, or the assistance of friends and relatives. Then what? One option is to seek analysis, if such a practice exists within reach, and time and funds or a supportive institution make this possible. It usually does not come cheap (given the frequency of meetings), even if analysts frequently charge far less per hour than is common in other professions (medicine or law for example).

The first destination for anyone suffering disabling psychological conditions nowadays might well be a visit to a doctor, then a referral to a psychologist or psychiatrist. Psychiatry was already established when Freud trained as a doctor, and he was well versed in it. Psychiatry is the medical speciality for the classification, diagnosis, and treatment of mental disorder; neurology, Freud's own early specialism, concerns the study and treatment of the nervous system and the disorders that affect it.

Different societies offer distinct choices. Where I am in London, treatment options are numerous. I could opt for one of the meditative techniques to enhance my well-being, exploring a myriad of mind–body approaches that carry an avowedly spiritual component, and which may be derived (more or less substantially) from elements of Buddhism and other religious practices. An approach known as 'mindfulness' is now increasingly popular in the West; generally conducted with groups, mindfulness courses usually last a relatively short duration, and encourage a person to take heed of thoughts and feelings, attend to sensations as they emerge in the body, and especially the unnoticed features of breathing. Here you might be helped to register passing thoughts but not run after them, and to live more meaningfully in the here and now. It is said to be highly effective in pain management. In earlier times, several other approaches to mind and therapy had also promised swifter and more positive results than Freudian analysis. These included Gestalt (as developed by Fritz Perls and his associates) and the techniques of 'person-centred therapy' (championed by Carl Rogers), which become popular in the 1960s.

There is no shortage of 'life coaches' and 'counsellors'. One prominent option today for the treatment of conditions like depression or acute anxiety is cognitive behavioural therapy (CBT), a treatment now widely adopted by health services in many countries. CBT emerged in the 1960s, the product of work by various clinicians, notably an American psychiatrist Aaron Beck. Disillusioned with psychoanalysis, Beck sought a more rapid method. He also took issue with behaviourism, another sometime rival to Freud's talking cure, which had found inspiration in the experiments of Pavlov (in Russia), and Watson (in the US). Behaviourists had imagined you could condition people to modify reprehensible and harmful actions; at its extreme, this approach treated human subjects as trainable creatures, barely more complex than dogs.

CBT focuses upon human behaviour while also concentrating upon engaging the patient's cognition. It is not really comparable to analysis—its focus of treatment and understanding is the *conscious* mind. Here the therapist works to identify difficulties and seeks to assist the client in tackling them, using reasoning to show how certain entrenched views are misconceived and can be circumvented. Such endeavours, in a different guise ('moral therapy'), had also gained traction during the 19th century when doctors and other healers sought to use 'common sense' to convince the mentally afflicted of their faulty logic, and to reason them back to health. CBT seeks to break problems down into components, discussing evidence for and against a given 'negative' belief, and may well advocate 'homework', techniques of positive thinking and strategies to avoid succumbing to the harmful assumptions and actions. CBT trainees are taught standardized procedures, although clearly personal qualities play a part. While this eschews Freud's focus on the unconscious, it could be argued that powerful unconscious processes are mobilized, even if denied.

CBT, its proponents might say, offers a no-nonsense, brisk route more efficient than analysis. Analytic critics of CBT might, in return, say that without steady exploration of unconscious conflicts, a person may just end up swapping one neurotic 'solution' for another, none the wiser about the real meaning and purpose of either their symptoms or character armour. Moreover, the CBT therapist may be merely a new idealized figure who is obeyed.

In the post-war period, the prominent psychologist and doyen of IQ testing Hans Eysenck spearheaded public criticism of psychoanalysis, claiming it offered no therapeutic benefit. However, various trials since then have in fact demonstrated in many instances the effectiveness of both analysis and forms of psychotherapy derived from it, in helping a person alleviate or cope with diverse conditions and symptoms, from panic attacks to chronic depression. Compared with enthusiasts for CBT, analysts, however, have been slower to subject their work to such studies, and have often proved wary, even extremely critical, of the entire enterprise of outcome testing per se, pointing to its reductive and often crudely utilitarian nature.

Psychoanalysis is not as influential as it once was, at least in post-war Britain, France, and especially the US, but it survives nonetheless as a substantial force, continuing both in its traditional form and in various offshoots and adaptations, some less intensive and thus less costly. In some parts of the world, notably Latin America, its influence in the later 20th century expanded substantially, even as it may have waned elsewhere.

Psychoanalysis then is a form of inquiry, a theory of mind, and a mode of treatment concerned, above all, with the unconscious mind. It became a movement and set of institutions, inspiring many, but also galvanizing numerous opponents. It is not a subject on which people tend to be neutral! Freud's ideas have also been applied to history, cinema, society, religion, management and business, drama, the dynamics of groups, and the exploration of ideologies.

Many insights in Freud's work have never been bettered; nonetheless, there have been major advances in theory and practice through the last century. Indeed, the findings not only of Freud but also of Klein, Bion, Winnicott, and Lacan (to name a few) provide a treasure house of clinical experience and ideas, models of the mind and of unconscious relationships, simply not available earlier in the history of the movement.

Critique of psychoanalysis and of its sub-movements has taken many forms. Sometimes disagreements spurred new ideas and modified techniques within the mainstream tradition. On other occasions, the challenges of some of Freud's early followers led to irresolvable differences and schisms. From the start, the movement was far more than the work of one man; it drew together many currents of thought, past and present. Psychoanalysis owed something to the philosophical ideas of Schopenhauer and Nietzsche. It was also paralleled and perhaps influenced, more than Freud ever cared to admit, by the work of other psychologists such as Pierre Janet in France, who had written extensively on the subconscious and furnished a host of clinical examples. Certainly ideas of this type were widely prevalent and diversely explored in *fin-de-siècle* Europe.

As the analytic movement expanded, Freud was especially indebted to trusted close associates and followers, such as Karl Abraham and Ferenczi. Undoubtedly, however, Freud was a giant of the discipline and remains the most widely recognized figure. Only one ally during his lifetime gained remotely comparable name recognition: Carl Jung, an illustrious younger colleague on whom Freud, for a time, pinned great hopes. Jung, however, fell out with Freud and left the movement (before World War I) to found his own distinct approach, commonly known as 'analytic psychology'.

This Very Short Introduction is neither a mini-intellectual biography, nor a detailed group portrait, nor again a stage-by-stage account of every path-breaking idea in analysis. My narrative moves freely between past and present, offering enough core history, I hope, to make contemporary approaches to analytical thought and to clinical practice intelligible.

Chapter 2
How psychoanalysis began

Psychoanalysis emerged between the 1880s and 1900s. Its origins can be traced to many sources; above all, to Freud's work on hysteria and dreams, his studies of everyday 'mistakes' (such as slips of the tongue or bungled actions), and inquiries into sexuality. The phrase 'talking cure', often used interchangeably with 'psychoanalysis', was coined before Freud's most important ideas had seen the light of day. A patient, Bertha Pappenheim (later to become a champion of women's education and rights), offered this description of her experience of treatment by Freud's colleague, Josef Breuer, in the early 1880s. Although it would be inaccurate to suggest that she ever fully recovered, she may well have gained some benefit. Her phrase captured an essential idea: Pappenheim had found relief in uncovering the first appearance of a particular symptom and in talking about the circumstances and early memories with her doctor.

Hysteria

At this time, diagnoses and treatments for Pappenheim's presumed condition (hysteria) were in flux. Doctors in search of new remedies experimented with approaches including hypnosis; they were intrigued, for example, to see if they could command a hypnotized patient to take on and then relinquish certain symptoms.

Pappenheim suffered a range of disabling problems, apparently without organic cause. She had a tendency to starve herself, displayed language disorders, and, at times, was paralysed. While some doctors still assumed that ultimately a physical explanation would be proved in this type of hysterical case, nobody could make sense of her stricken limbs and bouts of incapacity. During her treatment she was put into a trance. She would talk of her past, bringing up perturbing and previously inaccessible recollections and thoughts, not least concerning her dead father. This excavation, regarding what we might now call her relationships with her 'most significant others', seemed to help: a kind of emotional discharge occurred, and some of her symptoms were alleviated.

Freud too tried his hand at hypnotizing patients. He learned much about hysteria and hypnosis from two competing high-profile French doctors in the 1880s, Charcot and Bernheim. Freud absorbed what he witnessed during research visits abroad, but moved on from the practice of hypnosis. He focused increasingly on patients' language and its multiple meanings. He wanted the patient to be awake, speaking as freely as possible, and to show how the unconscious breaks through, seeking expression. Hysteria showed, for Freud, the dynamic struggles that take place within the mind.

Freud and Breuer argued in a joint publication in 1895 that hysterics suffered from conflicts concerning buried memories. Freud drew inspiration from Pappenheim's story and others like it, convinced that talking in a safe environment might enable patients to unravel disabling symptoms by bringing lost ideas, wishes, and fears to consciousness. Critics, however, have often expressed doubts that psychoanalysis ever fully broke free of the techniques of suggestion. They considered the analyst's charismatic hold to be an ominous aspect of the procedure, too easily trapping the patient in dependency, whatever Freud's claims about analysing, rather than exploiting, such unconscious states of mind. Freud himself remained ever interested in, and concerned about, the power of suggestion in all its guises, inside and outside the consulting room, and sought to understand its unconscious sources.

Certain memories and ensuing thoughts, Freud proposed, so horrified hysterical patients that they repressed them. In the 1890s he also developed the idea of free association, urging patients to try to act (as he put it some years later) 'as though [you are]... a traveller... sitting next to the window of a railway carriage and describing to someone inside the carriage the changing views which you see outside'. However, free association keeps getting interrupted, so a patient and analyst can potentially explore, in a session, the moment (to extend his analogy) when a blind is pulled down over the psychic window, closing off the view.

Pappenheim (or 'Anna O' as she was named in the literature in order—unsuccessfully—to disguise her identity) may have been enthusiastic, but her doctor, at least according to Freud's version, became less so; the story went that Breuer ended the sessions when he grew alarmed at her amorous wishes and thoughts *about him*. This was at a time when no psychoanalytic language was available to understand the unconscious emotional charge that can be reignited in the consulting room. In a major breakthrough, Freud would term this 'transference', showing our tendency unconsciously to carry over the baggage of the past into present relationships, thus 'investing' new figures with buried feelings, expectations, and beliefs. Analysis, he concluded, could be the place where the patient, with the analyst's help, might notice and thereby ultimately modify this transference pattern. Early emotional interactions, sometimes long repressed, are 're-experienced', but then, hopefully, can be grasped and better understood; few would argue now, however, that transference ever *fully* 'dissolves'. The handling of the transference, Freud observed, 'remains the most difficult as well as the most important part of the technique of analysis'.

Events and phantasy

It took Freud some time to draw together a theory of the significance of the sexual material that he and his colleagues were hearing when they listened to their patients. He first relied upon a particular hypothesis: the previously repressed thoughts in hysterics were unbearable early memories (stirred up again during adolescence) of sexual interference by another, perhaps a sibling, but often an adult member of the family or household. However, as case after case of such molestation and violation emerged, he came to doubt that real events were always necessarily the cause of the psychical trouble. He also pondered his own intermittent hysterical symptoms, while working on his 'self-analysis' (an attempt to investigate his buried thoughts, primarily by looking into his dreams).

Freud turned his focus increasingly to the subject's fears and phantasies. And he would emphasize repeatedly how complex, partial, and unreliable memories can prove: we reconstruct— skewing, adding, or subtracting—even as we strive to recall. While he did not deny the actual impact of others upon the self, this shift of emphasis in his own researches during the 1890s was marked: it might be, he argued, that the disturbing scene of 'rediscovered' sexual activity is in fact but a feature of the patient's own preoccupations.

Analysts have often returned to the question of the traumatic effects of family and environment. Much controversy surrounds the matter: how much weight to give nature or nurture, the inner world or the social field, the past or the present, in understanding ourselves? How do circumstances derail us, and how do we fashion, according to our own characters, the environment in which we live and the relationships upon which we rely? Vicious and virtuous circles can occur in the way people treat each other within families, as in larger groups. And psychic problems can sometimes play out across generations.

Freud also wrote at times about social groups, even whole societies, but he turned his main attention to the individual's unconscious, and the realm of phantasies. Some analysts use this 'ph' spelling specifically to indicate the unconscious form. For Freud, phantasy also suggested a link to the idea of mental 'play'. He even argued in a paper on creative writers and daydreaming in 1908 that we may mould ideas inside our minds, just as we once used toys, to create a make-believe world. The trouble is, he wrote, that 'people's phantasies are less easy to observe than the play of children'.

Freud was always interested in the *interaction* of mind and social circumstance, 'inner' and 'outer' realities. The fact that we may (as he so compellingly showed) be caught up in make-believe and reconfigure the past when our memories play tricks on us, should not, of course, ever be viewed as exonerating adults who actually abuse children, nor serve as a means of ignoring social hardship and material, as well as emotional, deprivation.

The brutal, uncertain, and terrifying environment endured by soldiers during World War I caused Freud and other analysts to take a further look at the relationship of internal and external reality, and to lay stress once more upon the consequences of life-shattering events. Evidence abounded that many men who had left for war fit and in good health returned as wrecks, racked by nightmares. It showed how circumstances could stir up our deep vulnerabilities, evoke, or re-evoke, raw terrors, and plunge us into states of unbearable guilt for surviving at all, when somebody else dies. Traumatic experiences can occur at any stage of life, certainly not only in earliest infancy or childhood.

Analysis has some broad, even universalizing theories, but also insists upon each individual's distinct psychic history and reactions to life. It concerns vagaries of personal existence, rejecting any notion that we are simply types. True, the analytic approach shows us that we face shared predicaments, such as what to make of mothers, fathers, friends, siblings, the ubiquitous problem of ageing and mortality, as well as narcissism. But each of us negotiates these matters in our own particular way. There are gaping divisions between pauper and king, yet as Shakespeare wrote, we all begin life by 'Mewling and puking in the nurse's arms', and we all face the prospect of an end, in 'second childishness and mere oblivion, | Sans teeth, sans eyes, sans taste, sans everything'. How each of us deals with such facts of life, which include the helplessness of babyhood and the inevitability of death, is another question. Analysis identifies and investigates common structures, but also reveals, to quote a phrase from the New Zealand-born analyst Joyce McDougall, countless possible 'theatres of the mind'.

Life and death, Freud proposed, confront us with divided feelings; we are, he takes it, bound to love and hate, want to know and not know, create and destroy, be active and inert. Mixed emotions are also inevitable towards the parental figures who brought us into being, and who usually bring us up: somehow we have to deal with ambivalence, the fact that we may both yearn for and hate the very same person or thing. This combination of feelings is powerfully evoked in the long and necessary struggle to separate and gain a sense of identity.

Freud's growing doubts about his first hypothesis (known, unfortunately, as 'the seduction theory') provided ammunition for later critics. He sometimes wrote incautiously of this early shift of perspective. Some have since claimed he took the (absurd) position that 'bad stuff' is confined to a world of the subject's unconscious imagining. It is not a question of either/or. But he did place conflicts within the mind at the heart of the *analytic* quest. The important point was that acts of gross and abusive kinds by adults upon children are not a *necessary* condition for hysteria.

This debate about what Freud got right and wrong in his shifting inquiries into neuroses and their causes never went away, and it also stimulated other clinicians to broaden their understanding of the implications of his ideas about 'seduction'. Much later, for example, the French analyst Jean Laplanche argued that all infants, not only those facing inadequate or malevolent carers, struggle to make something of the enigmatic meanings in adult desires. Babies and infants not only have sensations, but also encounter the mysterious pleasures and pains, wishes and sometimes hatreds of the adult in forms that cannot yet be 'read'. The actions and wishes of others are always partly opaque, but most especially in our early years we register without comprehending 'unmetabolized traces' of feelings and attitudes in the other.

Abuse, Laplanche proposed, needs to be thought about in relation to this broader problem of meaning, and the struggle we face to decipher other minds. We all must deal with the multiple legacies from early childhood, battling with emotions, beliefs, and identifications that may emerge, be buried, or recast at different moments. We have to form or forge identities from a myriad of different sources and influences.

The fact that adults can behave in an aggressive, exploitative, or sadistic manner does not mean the child necessarily sees them only as enemies to be hated and shunned. Victims of a tormenting figure might feel desperate to retain their love, may even idealize their tormentor (a situation often repeated later in life). Those who have been abused might also 'identify with the aggressor', a concept explored especially closely by Ferenczi and Anna Freud, who showed how patients might need to defend themselves in this way against unbearable feelings, associated with victimhood. By identification, analysts mean the way a person 'takes on' some aspect, property, or attribute of another. As Laplanche and Jean-Bertrand Pontalis put it in their invaluable glossary, *The Language of Psychoanalysis*, through identification, a subject may be 'transformed, wholly or partially, after the model the other provides'.

In analysis, patients bring residues of their pasts. In the process, they may remember things they had long forgotten, make new connections, or see old relationships in a different light. How 'there and then' relates to 'here and now', and what distortions occur in perception, are not just abstract questions—they can often be closely and meaningfully explored, with a particular patient, in a given session. There are related forms of psychotherapy involving work with couples or families, but in classical analysis the individual brings relationships and social networks only in the sense of talking about them, or perhaps at times (wittingly or otherwise) mimicking particular people or aspects of their minds, perhaps in order to convey to the analyst what they are like.

Reality and the unconscious

The unconscious, Freud claimed, contains some inherited contents that had never entered a person's awareness. His main concern, however, was with what was once known, or half glimpsed, and then actively pushed from consciousness. His account of the mind (1900), known as the topographical model, in the famous chapter 7 of *The Interpretation of Dreams* provided a theoretical starting point for analysis. In this model the main division is between conscious and unconscious, but in addition he also described the 'preconscious', in recognition of those thoughts and feelings that we *can* recall, but that are not in our direct awareness at the present moment. He also described an internal censor, filtering out or reshaping what is most unpalatable to the conscious self.

Analysis does not deny the force of material reality, independent of the mind. But it suggests that each of us is consciously and unconsciously constructing our own versions of our lives, past and present. We project mental contents into images of things 'out there', or into other people or particular situations, and then take these versions back inside. Reality is thus not something you view unadulterated. This contention is certainly not the unique preserve of psychoanalysis: many philosophers, novelists, and social theorists would agree with it. In short, there are many ways of seeing and not seeing, and no omniscient vantage point. Each of us perceives in an inimitable way, but it is through the shared realm of language that we put our world together and can find, and also lose, our sense of meaning.

Freud drew attention to times when we may lose track altogether of external constraints, our minds no longer taking heed of what he called 'the reality principle'. Operating, instead, according to the 'pleasure principle', we may live temporarily in a state of mind that gratifies, and seek to conjure the very thing we lack. When mothers are absent, infants may even hallucinate the breast or bottle. The advantage of the infant's thumb is that it can be sucked at will. Such substitutions can be both gratifying *and* frustrating. This capacity to dream up what is so painfully missing, at times, might be the only thing holding a person together.

However, this endeavour to follow the pleasure principle, which may in early life or in traumatic situations be crucially 'adaptive', can also become the expression of psychological difficulties—for example where we believe we have total command of the world, regardless of reality. Hallucination or wishful thinking only takes us so far. Freud wrote that reality breaks through when the infant, perhaps too hungry to make do, realizes that such self-fashioned images and substitutes also disappoint: the imagined food is not the real, nourishing thing.

The reality principle means acknowledging that everything cannot be permanently pleasant or under our thumb. Often we waver, as we try to accept postponements of wishes, come to terms with less than ideal outcomes, and face our own dependency and limits. An obdurate reality, sooner or later, looms up: in certain dreams we soar through space, and in infant games we might assume a role as superman or woman; but only a seriously manic, deluded, and/or disastrously intoxicated adult would attempt solo flight from a cliff and expect to survive.

Dreams

The creation of psychoanalysis depended upon several sets of ideas that crystallized, around the turn of the century; perhaps the most important was Freud's *Interpretation of Dreams*. He declared his method here the 'royal road' to knowledge of the unconscious activities of the mind and remarked of this work that such insight comes but once in a lifetime. The dreaming state, like the hypnotized state, can provide access to more forbidden thoughts, as there is a partial release from censorship. By Freud's lights, dreams are a compromise between the need to censor and the force of the unconscious that presses for expression. He observed how dreams serve an obvious function—helping us stay asleep; they also contain a host of thoughts and wishes, usually in camouflaged forms. To begin to unravel dreams Freud suggested that the dreamer give associations, allowing free play to the chain of thoughts subsequently evoked by each element from the scene.

One of Freud's own dreams provides a good example. He remembered from the dream a book that 'lay before me and I was at the moment turning over a folded coloured plate. Bound up in each copy there was a dried specimen of [a] plant, as though it had been taken from a herbarium.' This sounds a bit dry. But he then used the dream to uncover further thoughts and see how the unconscious weaves things together. He recalled how that morning he had seen a new book dealing with cyclamens, his wife's favourite flowers, and then feeling guilty (he so rarely remembered to bring such gifts, even though she liked them). He associated to a monograph he had written on the coca plant, which aimed to rival the work of other scientific investigators, concerning cocaine's anaesthetic properties. This train of thought sparked a theme concerned with illness and surgery. Freud recollected how his father had suffered glaucoma shortly after he (Sigmund) had been embroiled in that work on cocaine. He made a new link to the previous evening when he had been talking to

Professor Gartner (gardener in German) and had congratulated him and his wife on their blooming looks. Associations continued to blossom.

In each example, Freud used the immediate recollection to see what associations follow, to people and events, as well as to states of mind such as guilt, envy, ambition, and aggression. In this instance, the dream, which could be expressed in a few lines, generates numerous associations, requiring a much longer text. Even so, the associative chain, he thought, would hit some limit: this he termed the 'navel' of the dream, the point where it disappears into the interior, a completely unknowable dimension of oneself. The same applies in analysis. No analyst would claim that a patient ever has a 'complete' treatment, or fully unravels the meanings of thoughts and actions.

Dreams do more than just contain such jostling thoughts: they rework them. The dream also has a modicum of shape, corresponding, Freud proposed, to certain 'considerations of representability'. Crucially, this movement between the underlying thoughts and the dream's form is accomplished through what Freud called the *dream work*. That includes the unconscious capacity to dislodge one thing into another, or indeed to compress or condense together two (or more) items that may be quite at odds.

It would be quite wrong to imagine that everyone before Freud treated dreams as ephemeral. Many psychological theories and interpretations of dream life preceded psychoanalysis. Some, but not all, had viewed such phenomena as impositions from divine or demonic sources; it had been commonplace to view dreams as omens. Freud's work came in the wake of the Enlightenment; if he was interested in religious creeds, and in superstitions, his approach and style were insistently secular, and his work an attempted deep analysis, not an endorsement, of what he regarded as irrational subjective and social beliefs.

He was also particularly interested in 'the uncanny', albeit seeing his purpose, primarily, as scientific; Freud tended to take a wry and dis-enchanted view of the mind and the world, even while not discounting processes such as telepathy as necessarily fanciful. (Proud of and identified with his Judaism, and alert to anti-Semitism, Freud also described himself as a 'Godless Jew'.) He certainly did not view dreams as inspired predictions, nor celebrate them primarily as catalysts for artistic expression. Freud's interest here owed something to ideas promulgated by the Romantics, yet his method broke new ground, proposing a way to work over the contents of dreams, when subsequently awake, to learn more of our hidden psychic lives.

So dreams, he proposed, condense disparate thoughts; thus, the plant in that botanical dream pulls together different elements into a single scene. They also involve one word or image sliding sideways from or into another. While our more orderly thoughts follow certain conventions, sifting things out as ridiculous, in the unconscious normally antagonistic ideas co-reside. Disturbing, fantastical, or, to our waking minds, 'impossible' propositions may exist in dreams, with no apparent constraints of time.

There were inconsistencies: Freud discussed so-called 'typical dreams', a notion at odds with his main thesis. Here he reverted to a traditional view that dream symbols ultimately were shared and translatable regardless of the dreamer, a commonplace assumption in many Victorian dream books. But even superficially similar dreams from two patients, according to Freud's major argument, would diverge as soon as associations start to flow.

For Freud, dreams tell of hidden preoccupations and forbidden desires; his writings indicate how, nonetheless, analyst and patient could collaboratively explore what lies behind reveries and nightmares alike within the treatment. He developed here a larger thesis too, regarding the ubiquitous unconscious life of the mind, and used the phrase 'primary process' to indicate a free-flowing form of psychic activity, unconstrained by dictates of morality, time, or so-called common sense. This was in contrast to more organized conscious forms of thought and mental functioning that he named 'secondary process'. Furthermore, even riotous dreams may come to be 'secondarily revised' as we try to remember them, perhaps tidying them up to make a story and repressing anew elements that jar.

Freud never ceased exploring such processes, primary and secondary. His vision of the mind shows people always struggling to keep the lid on; we are caught between the pleasure-driven and often rather anarchic primary process on the one side, and the need to censor, constrain, and revise on the other. Often we do the latter in order to avoid confronting ourselves, or others, with too much scandal, pain, or anxiety. When awake we may in fact be most asleep to what is insistent in our unconscious.

Slips and jokes

In this early phase Freud also gathered jokes and yarns in which normally unspeakable, aggressive, or obscene thoughts are regarded permissively. Comedians in many cultures, after all, are allowed a certain licence. Jokes may bring home the absurd, and contain home truths.

Freud also particularly enjoyed the following Jewish story. Two Jews met in a railway carriage at a station in Galicia. 'Where are you going?' asked one. 'To Cracow', was the answer. 'What a liar you are!' broke out the other. 'If you say you're going to Cracow, you want me to believe you're going to Lemberg. But I know that in fact you're going to Cracow. So why are you lying to me?' Freud remarked upon the assertion of the first Jew that the second is dissembling when he tells the truth, and would be telling the truth by means of a lie.

The serious substance here is the problem of what determines truth and how we read between the lines; the story is pointing to a problem we have in knowing how to decipher what others *really* mean. Speech is shrouded in uncertainties and requires second guesses.

Freud seized equally enthusiastically upon those telling errors we all make, now referred to as 'Freudian slips'—occasions when, for instance, we inadvertently blurt out something embarrassing and consciously unintended. An impressively candid teacher at my school many years ago offered this example, when asked to explain what Freud had in mind: once, talking to an attractive group of final year girls, who were protesting at his harsh marks for an exam, the teacher impulsively retorted, 'be quiet, or I'll go lower and take far more off all of you right now'.

A double-entendre, or a slip, might at times reveal something we are aware of and don't want to reveal; at others, an idea we are not cognizant of in the first place. In 2014, the press reported British Conservative Prime Minister David Cameron's revealing misreading: in referring to poor children on council estates, he insisted: 'these are the people we resent'. On his autocue was the word 'represent'. Even Conservative newspapers dubbed it a 'Freudian slip'. This was the kind of terrain amply explored in Freud's *The Psychopathology of Everyday Life* (1901). Blunders, no less than dreams, are entirely commonplace: here again Freud insistently shifted attention from unusual psychopathologies to shared human experience.

Sexuality

Freud's writings on sexuality in the early 1900s were arguably as noteworthy as his work on dreams. His discussion of sexuality came at the end of an important cluster of research in the late Victorian period by campaigners for less prudish education and medical enlightenment. Energetic doctors and researchers such as Richard von Krafft-Ebing and Havelock Ellis investigated the diversity of sexual behaviour, helping establish a field of inquiry that came to be called 'sexology'. These explorers sought to move discussion of sex away from prurience or pornography to dispassionate, scientific ground. Some of these contributions eschewed religious strictures only to create medico-psychiatric norms, upholding a firm distinction between the 'ill' and the 'healthy'. But the endeavour to discuss sexual desires and behaviour frankly, at least between fellow physicians, was striking. Freud sought to be equally plainspoken with patients.

There has been much debate about whether the Victorians were really as sexually repressive as popular convention has had it. But either way, the psychoanalytical approach proposed that tolerating the expression of the normally unsayable, in the consulting room, might prove helpful and liberating, as well as anxiety-provoking. Some analysts, such as Klein, built on Freud's work and sought to show what a relief it could be for even the youngest child patients to be permitted to express their most anxious, excited, or murderous thoughts, and be listened to openly without strictures to 'mind your tongue'.

In *Three Essays on the Theory of Sexuality* (1905) Freud set the scene, considering in detail infantile psychosexual development, the torment of discordant feelings, and the manner of their repression. He was particularly interested to understand what in sexuality is irreducible to biological functions. Freud certainly shared in the commitment to viewing people as biological creatures, and endorsed evolutionary theory (even offering some speculations of his own). But in describing the vicissitudes of human desire, he moved in a different direction to one of his heroes, Darwin, who had focused upon instinctual aspects of sexual selection and the mechanisms of animal descent.

For Freud, we are animals with a difference; we are faced with our own—and other people's—unconscious minds, and we find ourselves propelled by often highly ambiguous 'drives'. By this term he meant forces inside a person that lie on the cusp between the biological and the psychological. These are not fixed in aim or goal. A drive may find an object of some kind to meet it, but which object and what form the drive may take is not pre-set. Instinct, by contrast, implies a hereditary pattern of response typical of a species.

The upshot of Freud's account was the recognition that we all struggle to deal with the confusions of our early development, and with the propulsive and uncertain qualities of the drives. Freud took it that we are all bisexual to begin with. Each person finds sexual 'solutions' of some kind—for example, the mantle of celibacy, monogamy, adultery, promiscuity, or an identity as 'gay', 'straight', or 'bi'—but not without traversing excitements and terrors, compromises and repressions, bound up with early infantile states. Freud used the term 'libido' to mean sexual interest or appetite, but also to add a broader sense of the underlying energy in all those feelings we group together under 'love'. It might refer to affection as well as lust, or describe certain powerful emotions that bind groups and communities.

Psychoanalysis suggests how sexuality involves a host of different feelings that may be enjoyed, endured, subdued, or displaced; it has, for Freud, a powerfully excessive and thus potentially troubling quality. There are multiple ways to feel and there are also diverse states of mind we encounter in others—states with which we might identify ourselves, or pit ourselves against. Each person may ascribe a variety of meanings and purposes, conscious and unconscious, to sexual intercourse for example. In the unconscious, one person may well stand in for someone or something else.

Freud's work on sexuality is important not least because it suggests the limitations of conventional and generic labels, such as, say, 'a monogamous couple' or 'a repressed homosexual' to describe complex, idiosyncratic identities and processes. Analysis is always, by definition, a journey into the unknown. The talking cure invites, precisely, the exploration of unconscious psychic life, and investigates what we may unknowingly seek from ourselves, and from others.

Infancy and childhood

The infant, Freud thought, experiences the most intense pleasure, disappointment, and pain. The skin, smell, gaze, the act of suckling, or even excreting, and body warmth can yield a dividend of psychic enjoyment. Particular body parts, most notably mouth, anus, and genitals, become the source of special preoccupation. Too neatly perhaps, he imagined a standardized chronological course: oral, anal, phallic, latency, and genital 'stages' of development.

While some found this shocking, even disgusting, many of Freud's contemporaries were deeply impressed by his approach: for example, his bold exploration of how finance and faeces might have notable subliminal connections. The famous economist John Maynard Keynes is a case in point: he was among those greatly taken by Freud's arresting argument that for each of us economics and politics might be marked by the most visceral feelings, for example about incorporating piles of goods and expelling unwanted things. Keynes could see how money itself could be invested with very powerful unconscious attitudes of one kind or another.

How psychoanalysis began

In his account of sexuality and development, Freud gave primacy to the male. In the phallic stage, for both sexes, the key issue is the presence or absence of the penis, rather than an equal reciprocal awareness of bodily difference. (Later, he would also explore in some detail how people could get hooked on fetish objects, for instance shiny boots, and give women special phallic power, in order to evade awareness of sexual difference or, in Freud's terms, the woman's lack of a penis.)

The phallic phase is followed by a period he called latency, especially marked by embarrassment and shame, when the sexual dimension tends to be disavowed, or at least appears less immediately apparent. All this culminated in a genital stage that

37

is exceptionally marked in puberty, when sexual feelings come to be more focused. Preoccupation with genitalia, he surmised, is already clearly evident in infancy and childhood, but in adolescence sexuality tends to be linked in a new way with 'the service of reproduction' and thus with the organs concerned in that. But Freud complicated this account, stressing that a more supposedly adult (genital) sexuality is never free of pre-genital aspects (for instance, oral pleasures).

Many traces of infantile experience and meaning persist— yearnings for instance, to kiss, stroke, and hug; but much of our early delight *and* dismay is also repressed. Freud thus strongly insisted that children are not immune to or innocent of the sexual; elements of this more diffuse infantile sensuality and intense passion may persist through life, whatever our conscious sexual identities, or indeed capacities, as he put it, successfully to *sublimate* erotic feelings. Examples of sublimation—those occasions when we might deflect or subsume sexual feelings into other, sometimes 'higher' purposes—could include absorbing ourselves in works of art or music, feats of sport, treatises in philosophy, or even developments in psychoanalytical thought.

For Freud, earliest infancy brings with it a host of 'polymorphous' pleasures. He wryly called that pleasure 'perverse', thus bringing what had been a category of the abnormal (as when people talk about 'the pervert') into uncomfortably close proximity with the everyday and 'normal'. This was not to sanction 'anything goes' behaviour in adulthood, nor to assume everybody's phantasies are identical, but to recognize we remain affected, even afflicted, by our own most archaic thoughts, anxieties, and desires, and sometimes project them into others. We might well prefer to attribute our chaotic or outrageous feelings, for example, exclusively to some special class of deviant.

Some, Freud argued, become fixated—stuck at a particular stage of development. His account implied a certain unfolding sequence, as well as a capacity to stall or regress. And just as infants may triumphantly experience newfound mastery of bodily sphincters, so adults might seek to create a world in which everything is putatively under control. The plot thickens; Freud added another idea, 'reaction formations'. An obsession with 'tidying up' might bear traces of the dirty anal preoccupations it seeks to shut out. One thing may perturbingly be revealed to symbolize another. Moreover, adults are often left struggling with fears and phantasies they were supposed to have left behind in childhood. In Chapter 3 we consider such a case.

Chapter 3
A case of obsessional neurosis

In early autumn 1907, a youngish man of university education, Mr R, made an appointment to see Freud at Berggasse 19, Vienna. This was Freud's home and office for most of his working life, the hub within which analysis developed. R was plagued with worries about the consequences of his thoughts and wishes, which he found hard to distinguish from deeds. He believed that his mind was sometimes completely transparent; this was apparent to him in youth, when he suspected that his parents could see right into him. R told Freud about the endlessly self-torturing doubts he faced and of his despair: among his more alarming compulsions was an impulse to cut his own throat with a razor. R had already tried other remedies, without success, for the illness that was sapping the life out of him.

Spurred by what he had read and heard of Freud, R began an analysis. Freud wrote about him in one of his *case histories*, those extended examples of a treatment. This particular patient (known simply, and perhaps unfortunately, just as 'The Rat Man') is described in 'Notes Upon a Case of Obsessional Neurosis' (1909). The text runs on at great length, almost as though this patient's obsessions became Freud's own.

No sooner had R entered the room, than he was making assumptions about the analyst and using sessions in complex and conflicted ways that could potentially be analysed. Freud recorded, for example, how R made implicit evaluations about what this latest clinician would be most interested to hear, and seemed agonized about what he could or could not say. The spectre of punishment also quickly shadowed proceedings. There were details R assumed Freud should be told; others he preferred to keep secret or defer. R already knew of the sexual theories analysis advanced; he obligingly furnished some data about his sexual history, such as the observation that his potency was 'normal', and a revelation about the first date at which he had sexual intercourse (other matters, however, stuck in his throat). R also soon told Freud about a one-time student and friend who offered to tutor him; he explained that this man had ulterior motives, using contact with R to get to know his sister. He conveyed his disappointment at this discovery.

It is worth using this example to consider as well how analytic practice has since changed. Freud or any analyst following would have probed meanings like the very particular significance that the sister and tutor held. A practitioner today, however, might well be more attentive than Freud was then to the potential unconscious implications of such statements *within the analysis*. Opinion today is divided about how best to talk about and interpret the patient's past—how helpful and necessary it is to try, as Freud did, to root out the exact combination of history and phantasies a patient may have lived with years before treatment, and how far it is useful for the analyst to spell out what the patient may be feeling, thinking, or doing in the present moment of the treatment. But most would agree that this dimension of 'here and now' should at least be kept in mind, even when the analyst and patient are exploring traumatic events outside the room, or long ago.

R, as noted, had told of a difficult and unexpected triangular situation in which he was betrayed: patient, 'friend', and a third party. In his 'transference' to Freud, might we then see an analogy with his story? Did he perhaps fear that Freud, like the false-friend

41

tutor, would use him for some other purpose than the overt one too, and betray him for the sake of something or someone else?

One key incident, to emerge later in the analysis, was a severe beating R had endured as a child at the hands of his father. This was when he had been 'naughty', or, Freud suspected, caught masturbating. The boy had flown into a rage so intense during this punishment that his father backed off, never to repeat the beating. The sense of a child being beaten, however, and the threat of a violent attack ensuing upon the punitive father, never really went away. Freud found 'the unconscious complement' of this formative moment of R's life when the patient, otherwise respectful, began heaping 'the filthiest abuse upon me and my family', before inviting the analyst, as it were, to hit back: 'How can a gentleman like you, sir,' he used to ask, 'let yourself be abused in this way by a low, good-for-nothing fellow like me? You ought to turn me out: that's all I deserve.'

Curiosity and punishment

R was concerned that a thought, such as the anticipation of his father's death, might lead to its realization. He faced harsh internal accusations about his own hatefulness, especially in recognizing some wish for that death. He could not bear his own ambivalence. Freud suggested to the reader how R's covetous wishes towards women and fear of his own destructiveness were also closely connected, so any inquiry—and analysis itself—carried dangers: looking and destroying were bound up together. R's sexual curiosity, Freud found, was enmeshed with his murderous thoughts about his father. Another story R revealed concerned a governess; during his childhood, she had allowed him to look under her skirt on condition he did not tell. He was not satisfied by such glimpses; his desire to look continued unabated, yet he dreaded the consequences. Indeed, R was tormented by the thought: 'If I have this wish to see a woman naked, my father will be bound to die.'

Freud was surprised to discover that the father in question had already passed on. It was surprising, presumably, not least because R *senior* appeared to be so entirely alive in his patient's mind. R was fearful of killing him over and over. Here one might recall *Hamlet*, a play dear to all analysts, in which the spectre of the dead (or murdered) father haunts the son, plays upon his mind, demands action, and evokes guilt: 'I am thy father's spirit | Doom'd for a certain term to walk the night', says the ghost to Hamlet.

R felt guilty, and deeply—if largely unconsciously—consumed by his own responsibility for events he had not actually caused. A few months before his father's death, R revealed, it had occurred to him that being rid of his old man would make him rich enough to marry; we learn how besotted and confused he was by conflicted thoughts of a woman referred to as 'his lady', and about benefiting from his father's death. At the same time he also felt defenceless, convinced others saw right into him, attacking him back.

The cruel captain

R spoke to Freud of his experiences in the army, particularly conversations with a cruel captain, who revealed an unspeakable form of oriental punishment. Freud surmised that R was horrified *and* excited by a particular sadistic scenario: 'a horror at pleasure of which he was unaware'. In this punishment a pot containing rats was turned upside down over the buttocks of a tied-up prisoner; these creatures, upon release, burrowed their way into the victim's body through . . . 'the anus'; Freud had to say the last words, for R fell silent at the moment of reaching for them.

R was unable to get those thoughts out of his head or, unaided, the words from his mouth. On prompting, the word 'rat' precipitated a host of associations; a remarkable carrier of meanings, not just a sign indicating a rodent. Before describing this horrible scene of the rat entering the anus, R had begged Freud to free him from the obligation to speak his mind on this subject. Freud replied—firmly—that he could just as well promise the moon, since the requirement is for the patient to attempt freely to speak his thoughts, however unpleasant.

Again, we can see how the story that a patient tells *in an analysis* can resonate with possible unconscious meanings ascribed *to the analysis*. R's expectations of relationships frequently involved scenarios involving cruelty and punishment, as well as excitement, fear, and remorse. A part of R's mind was apparently enjoying this picture of cruelty even while another looked on askance. Consider too how this reluctant, tongue-tied patient asked for forbearance, only for the analyst to press, even command—nudged, perhaps, to do so by R.

Freud was also at pains to tell the patient that his (i.e. the analyst's) own intentions were not at all like those of the captain—he was analysing, not tormenting; and made clear he took no pleasure in participating in stories of cruelty. The gist was that Freud was dispassionate, as scientist and therapist. Yet could the analyst have begun to figure in the same scenario R was talking about—a new cruel 'officer' to punish and gratify, as he lay, like a prisoner, on the couch? Had R perhaps even keyed into something unconsciously zealous, or even a bit cruel, in his analyst?

Freud recounted the way these near unspeakable thoughts went round in the patient's mind, as he imagined ghastly retribution inflicted upon a male prisoner, like his father, or even upon the enthralling lady. The punishment, R insisted defensively, was carried out 'impersonally'; such matters were 'entirely foreign and repugnant to him'. Both Freud and R disavowed any intention of cruelty or any personal connection to the punishing scenario. R was often aghast at what emerged in his analysis: 'He wondered how he could possibly have had such a wish [to kill off his parent], considering that he loved his father more than any one else in the world.'

Psychic work

Analysis, Freud indicated in a footnote to this case, is not *meant* to be about persuading or cajoling people to dig out the truth; better let them work things out in their own time, albeit with the analyst's help. He later developed a concept—working through—that captured such a process of therapeutic collaboration which involved both patient and analyst alike. In this way a new and difficult idea might be assimilated, truly implanted in the patient's mind, thereby overcoming resistance.

This point about the patient's need to work things out, over, or through is important. For Freud did, on occasion, push his patients hard, and show how much he was the one in the know, the truth-seeker. But the patient can only gain a true sense of conviction, Freud wrote, when he 'has himself worked over the reclaimed material... and so long as he is not fully convinced the material must be considered as unexhausted'. In another footnote, added long after the first publication of *The Interpretation of Dreams*, Freud declared that psychoanalytic technique 'imposes the task of interpretation upon the dreamer himself',

Ego, id, and superego

Regardless of official beliefs (or lack thereof), we construct our own gods and demons, or 'cruel captains', living under our own dark skies, caught between conflicting voices and choices. Indeed, by Freud's lights none of us is as consistent as we like to suppose. Those of secular opinion, even card-carrying atheists, can still believe in retribution, even for a passing wish. Conflicting impulses, Freud suggested, might have roots in *unconscious* attitudes, quite different from those knowingly maintained.

In 1923, Freud came up with a model that gave a new, and some would argue sharper, form to his picture of the mind, referring to an internal agency that watches and judges. As so often, his new concepts were inspired by clinical phenomena; they were attempts to grasp the complexities of what he faced in the consulting room. He had previously given many intimations of such unconscious reproaches that took place inside people; now he formalized this aspect and called it 'the over I', or, in the standard translation, the superego. Its strength and harshness, according to psychoanalysis, is an important determinant of well-being or mental ill health.

Freud also posited two other agencies here: ego and id. The ego is in one sense the part of the mind that perceives and 'mediates' internal and external reality. Freud spoke of it, however, as a 'poor creature owing service to three masters, and consequently menaced by three dangers': the external world, the superego, and what he called *das Es*, 'the it', a term rendered in English (by recourse to Latin, which made it sound more formal) as the id. This is a wholly unconscious part of the mind that contains instinctual urges and passions. Freud placed the id at the bottom of a diagram he drew of the mind, underneath the ego. But it does not stay submerged; it can erupt and overtake us, like an alien force within.

Freud stressed the presence of basic sexual and aggressive drives in the id; and noted a certain capacity of the ego for perception. 'The ego', he wrote, 'represents what may be called reason and common sense, in contrast to the id, which contains the passions.... Thus in its relation to the id [the ego] is like a man on horseback, who has to hold in check the superior strength of the horse.' Freud went on trying to define ego and id in various ways, but always with a sense of the divisions within us. Freud once declared that the intention of analysis is 'to strengthen the ego, to make it more independent of the super-ego, to widen its field of perception and enlarge its organization, so that it can appropriate fresh portions of the id'.

Neither id nor superego can be dissolved, but may perhaps be harnessed and tolerated in a less destructive manner. The superego can be violently demanding and critical, setting up the most exalted ideals to live up to. Freud referred to the 'ego ideal', meaning that imagined figure we would like to be if only we could. For some, the superego may be mostly mild, allowing some leeway to live and let live; for others it is an incessant, even sadistic scourge, creating feelings of worthlessness and abjection. Various later analysts, such as Bion, sought to show how, in some mad states, it may even serve to destroy the ego.

Analysis is a place to explore and discover, among other things, the particular timbre and character of the superego. It might be that the patient talks highly critically, or that the superego is projected into someone else. Thus the analyst may find herself treated as an auxiliary berating voice, while the patient seems to be appealing for clemency, or acting delinquently. Many pictures of self and other can exist at once: you may envisage yourself in phantasy, as craven, small, frightened of doing wrong, and yet be identified simultaneously with an all-powerful tribunal doling out punishment. In a psychotic form, this might be the condition of a person convinced of being Napoleon, before cowering in the corner terrified.

Different impulses and defences co-reside at any given time. Indeed, Herbert Rosenfeld, or more recently still John Steiner, show how defences are often formed into complex clusters, rather than operating one at a time. Patients may use a variety of *forms* of defence all at once, and indeed develop 'psychic retreats' to shelter within, or be crippled by elaborate 'pathological organizations' of the mind. These can require a person's silent and deadly acquiescence. Rosenfeld famously likened such states of mind to a mafia-style operation within.

R faced a desperate internal situation, and was also incredulous, as his analysis unfolded, that he could be so encumbered by thoughts and driven to actions that defied rational sense. Freud encouraged him to encounter openly his own unconscious wishes to hurt, murder, and magically restore loved ones all at once. Freud mentioned R's family and other associates in this narrative, but it was clear his father was the dominant figure. How far this faithfully reflected the patient's self-presentation, or Freud's prior assumptions about what matters, is debatable. We learn little of R's mother. Either way, Freud's focus is upon the patient's mental world, rather than any detail of the history or real attributes of his family or of the elusive 'lady'.

On the day of his lady friend's departure, R knocked his foot against a stone in the road, and then felt obliged to put it out of the way when the idea struck him that her carriage would be driving along in a few hours' time. She might come to grief if her vehicle hit this stone—something both wanted, to punish her for leaving, and dreaded (as he still had loving feelings towards her). So he changed his mind, compelled to do the opposite—an oscillation between love and hate that is common in obsessional states.

Freud went to extraordinary lengths to grasp the ideas behind R's apparently nonsensical activities, to trace his psychic history and to understand how obsessional doubts governed his life. How much the patient benefited from the treatment we cannot be sure, though Freud claimed it did him much good. A brief footnote added in 1923 states that the young man, like so many of his generation, died in World War I.

Chapter 4
Oedipus

Ever since Freud formulated the Oedipus complex, wrote the analyst Hanna Segal, 'it has been recognized as the central conflict in the human psyche—the central cluster of conflicting impulses, phantasies, anxieties and defences. It has therefore become the centre of psychoanalytic work.' It is indeed a pivotal idea in psychoanalysis, and one that has also been the source of withering criticisms.

Freud's ideas about Oedipus garnered enormous cultural interest and admiration too; for many it became an organizing model and a key to self-revelation. When Woody Allen created a sketch, 'Oedipus wrecks', for the movie *New York Stories*, the Freudian reference to the unfortunate King (Rex) and the condition to which he gave his name could be lightly assumed: Allen expects the audience to 'get it'. No doubt there would be puzzlement in some parts of the world about the joke, but the Oedipus complex must be among the most famous psychological ideas of the 20th century. The *New Statesman* magazine may have oversold Freud when it opined in the 1920s that 'we are all psychoanalysts now', but it captured nonetheless the excitement that was provoked by such core ideas from the talking cure.

This story begins in the 1890s, the period in which Freud was rethinking hysteria. In fact, Freud concluded, the two issues—hysteria and Oedipal wishes—are related. In 1926, he wrote of how obsessional compulsions and hysterical symptoms might stem from 'the necessity of fending off the libidinal demands of the Oedipus complex'. It was not the wishes, so much as the desperate quest to be rid of them altogether that caused the most trouble.

Small children do sometimes say out loud that one day they will marry mummy or daddy, before the penny drops that they cannot; even the expression of this wish may in some families be regarded as unacceptable. But whether or not the desire can be articulated freely, we all have to deal during infancy with the knowledge that enacting it would be impossible, and profoundly taboo. Freud found his inspiration in Greek myth: there you saw what happened when the gods permitted paternal murder and incest between son and mother to run their course: the result was tragedy.

The fate of Oedipus, set out in Sophocles' dramas, formed part of a larger network of myths. Freud explored the plot and took it as a useful means of understanding interior life: a baby cast out into the world, or here actually abandoned to die by its parents (convinced that thereby they would prevent a foretold disaster), surprisingly survives, is cared for by others, and eventually returns, unwittingly, in the direction of the very place from which he had been ejected. It is fated that Oedipus will meet and kill his father, blind to the knowledge of whom he is fighting; he is also destined to marry and sleep with his mother, oblivious about (or at least turning a 'blind eye' to) whom he is coupling with, thereby producing children who are both siblings and progeny. To deny vital differences between generations in this way brings catastrophe, whichever way around that denial occurs. Parents and children eventually have to let each other go.

This ancient story of the murder of the father and union with the mother—or alternatively matricide and union with the father—has such power, Freud suggested, because it resonates with a psychic truth about archaic states of mind in all of us. It horrifies us, he thought, because it is so close to the bone. Variations of the story of incestuous disaster often come back to haunt us, even when Freud's name is not invoked. Indeed, certain grotesque crimes have been much in the news lately, leading to renewed debates about the damage inflicted upon a person when Oedipal desire, or its reverse (the parent who seeks totally and brutally to possess the child as their thing) is enacted in psychotic form. At the very extreme was the monstrous case that came to light in Austria in 2008, of Elisabeth Fritzl, held in a secret dungeon for more than twenty years and repeatedly raped by her father, Josef. The daughter's babies born into this nightmare captivity were her siblings.

When Oedipus's wife and mother learned what had happened between them, she killed herself. He stabbed out his eyes with her brooch. Even then the tragedy was not complete: it resonated across generations. Freud wrote to a friend, Wilhelm Fliess, in 1897:

> the Greek myth seizes on a compulsion that everyone recognizes because he has felt traces of it in himself. Every member of the audience was once a budding Oedipus in phantasy, and this dream-fulfilment played out in reality causes everyone to recoil in horror, with the full measure of repression which separates his infantile from his present state.

Freud sought to give a rough periodization, suggesting these desires reach their most intense phase for a child between the ages of three and five. This he considered a period of crisis and transition, involving loss, anxiety, and guilt. How we meet or seek to evade the task of 'moving on' is relevant, Freud argued, to many aspects of mental functioning. The negotiation of the Oedipus complex, so it was claimed, shapes the way we relate to others and assume that others relate to us.

Analysts continue to use Freud's Oedipal account; the model provides a vantage point through which to explore, for instance, how certain jealousies, wishes, and counter-wishes about possessing parents or feeling dispossessed by them may be stirred up later in life, including in analysis. Oedipus also offers us a means of conceptualizing infantile psychic development. Subsequent work with children provided evidence to support and to complicate Freud's assumptions. Klein, for example, believed that these conflicts and desires appeared much earlier than Freud had assumed.

Criticism

A sense that something was missing, or misconceived, in the original account led to challenges as well as subsequent elaborations. The Oedipus complex offers a model to look at one aspect of psychic life, but by privileging it analysts arguably risk missing or underestimating other considerations.

As the analyst Juliet Mitchell has recently suggested, this focus may have led people to pay too little heed to the psychic significance of siblings, real and imagined; the traumas of displacement and loss for the existing child when a new baby arrives, and sibling desire for each other, are perhaps less well theorized than the 'vertical' relationship to parents, although, admittedly, the 'horizontal' relationship had appeared in many earlier analytic contributions too, for example in a suggestive paper in 1950 by Bion entitled 'The Imaginary Twin'.

Freud's model aroused admiration for its stark simplicity, and continuing criticism for its limitations and blind spots. In the 1920s, the anthropologist Malinowski, who respected Freud, also famously disputed his universalizing claims about the Oedipus complex, writing of cultures with very different kinship systems to those psychoanalysis assumed as standard. Freud's defenders, such as Ernest Jones, argued that the underlying predicament was not in fact so different, whether it might be a father, an uncle, or some other figure representing the key anchor point, beyond the mother, in the life of the infant.

Among the most stirring critiques of Freud's theory was *Anti-Oedipus* (1972) by the French philosopher Gilles Deleuze and analyst Felix Guattari. It argued, among other things, that Freud created a kind of 'Holy Family', no less constricting than old, religious versions of the same. This 'daddy–mummy–me' triangle (Freud's 'referential axis', as they put it) was a highly ideological imposition, constraining the multiplicity of human possibilities into a single, 'dreary' scheme. Oedipus, they declared, was a psychological imperialism, with the analysts enacting the very thing they described: the remorseless 'law of the father'. The story of desire, they pointed out, could be written in countless other ways. In short, they refused to accept Freud's Oedipal account. Some critics of these critics (including analysts stung by direct mockery of them in Deleuze and Guattari's writings) accused them in turn of enacting, like some other rebels of the 1968 student movement calling for the overthrow of the state, an infantile 'revolt against the father'.

The primal scene

In considering infantile sexuality and the Oedipus complex, Freud not only made the point that we can feel included or left out, but also that we acquire, early on in life, particular assumptions about our parents' sexual relations. Indeed, a vision of their sexual act, Freud thought, comes to be repressed. 'Primal scene' is the shorthand analysts use to mean the basic idea or image of parental intercourse that exists in somebody's mind, whether or not they have witnessed or heard their mother and father's sexual activity directly. For example, is the intercourse imagined as fundamentally loving, mutually enjoyed, hated by one or both, or primarily aggressive and sadistic in intent?

In a landmark text, *From the History of an Infantile Neurosis*, Freud described such a primal scene in the mind of a patient dubbed the 'Wolf Man'. This aristocratic Russian, whose real name became widely known, had arrived for analysis with Freud in

Vienna in 1910, his life severely shadowed by depression and other psychological problems. It was in his exploration of this patient's terrifying dream, featuring wolves sitting in a walnut tree, that Freud elaborated what he meant by the 'primal scene' (see Box).

The patient's associations, Freud suggested, in terse fashion, led towards a particular moment: 'A real occurrence—dating from a very early period—looking—immobility—sexual problems—castration—his father—something terrible'. Working over W's associations, they arrived at the rudimentary image of the parents' intercourse. In this particular case, the sexual act, which the patient linked to castration, apparently took place with the tiny child present in the room. His father was standing behind his mother, a position that gave their intercourse, for this patient at least, a more animal-like aspect. Freud speculated that W saw his

The Wolf Man's dream

I dreamt that it was night and that I was lying in my bed. (My bed stood with its foot towards the window; in front of the window there was a row of old walnut trees. I know it was winter when I had the dream, and night-time.) Suddenly the window opened of its own accord, and I was terrified to see that some white wolves were sitting on the big walnut tree in front of the window. There were six or seven of them. The wolves were quite white, and looked more like foxes or sheep-dogs, for they had big tails like foxes and they had their ears pricked like dogs when they pay attention to something. In great terror, evidently of being eaten up by the wolves, I screamed and woke up. My nurse hurried to my bed, to see what had happened to me. It took quite a long while before I was convinced that it had only been a dream; I had had such a clear and life-like picture of the window opening and the wolves sitting on the tree. At last I grew quieter, felt as though I had escaped from some danger, and went to sleep again.

parents' genitalia while they had sex, and that this was frightening, as though mother's body was mutilated, their physical contact brutal. It supported the patient's 'conviction that castration might be more than an empty threat'. Castration, in the analytic context, means not only literally the fear of the disfigurement or removal of the testicles, but the dread of a punitive attack on the genitals, or, more symbolically, a traumatic reduction, even entire incapacitation and annihilation.

This case study provided a complex scheme to explain the layers of meaning associated with that primal scene over time: only in the light of later knowledge and understanding could W make some sense of what he had first witnessed at the age of eighteen months. The image was frequently stirred up, imbued retroactively with new meanings and interest. Freud called this effect *Nachträglichkeit*. It has been translated as 'deferred action' or 'afterwardness', and in French as '*après coup*'.

Freud suspected that the terrifying dream, associated with bestial appetites, contained not only fragments of memory from W's early life, but also depictions of animals copulating witnessed elsewhere grafted on to the scene. Increasingly, this became linked to W's own obsessions and desires. Freud noted that something in this scenario was both frightening and arousing to W. Analytic interest lies in what a person, as here, makes of their own primal scene, what kind of phantasy it contains, and what, *après coup*, comes to be associated with it.

W remained in contact with Freud after his treatment stopped. Indeed, he became the most celebrated, although among the more enduringly unhappy, of Freud's former patients, and one who seemed in the end to belong to the psychoanalytic community and be cared for by it. Freud helped him financially during hard economic times. He had further analysis with Freud's disciples too, but remained beset by problems including bouts of severe melancholia. He spoke later in interviews with some suspicion

and bitterness of his experiences with Freud. Perhaps he gave
to psychoanalysis in the end as much as, or more than,
he obtained in return, not least by inspiring Freud's
conceptualization of deferred action and the primal scene.

Freud's account of the Oedipus complex and the primal scene has
also been taken up in many different kinds of inquiries, not just
concerning patients' pasts or phantasies about their analysts
during treatment, but also, for instance, regarding public curiosity
to discover the latest news about the trysts of so-called celebrities
and power couples, young and old. (Judging by the literature,
many have also wanted to read about Freud's own sex life, or the
lack of it, intent on knowing for sure whether he was faithful to
his wife, or had an affair with his sister-in-law, as rumour has it.)

Children are, of course, often intently curious about where they come
from and how they were made, and may well be simultaneously
squeamish about the nature of their parents' love lives. Getting the
distance right can be difficult. In some families the very mention of
sex may be excruciatingly taboo. But what more embarrassing fate for
teenagers, however liberal the household, than witnessing steamy sex
scenes at the cinema in the company of their mothers or fathers? It is
most likely the proximity of the parents, rather than the film alone, or
even at all, that makes them uncomfortable. Parents too may well
squirm, of course, at looking on in such company.

Breaking away

Freud places the boy's story centre stage, although the primary loss
of the enveloping mother, inside whose body every new life begins,
is shared equally by both sexes. Freud took up first the situation of
an infant (boy) who imagines he is the exclusive object for mother,
and she his. The illusion must be broken, the child obliged to cede
this imagined place and come to recognize that it was never, in
fact, quite his to start with: he is faced with the fact that he is part
of a triangle, not simply fused, or even in a dyad. Arguably the

full-blown version of the complex is but the end point of many earlier shocks, including the disturbance a baby may feel when the mother even inches away. One of Freud's followers, Otto Rank, had made much of the trauma of birth; others such as Klein and Winnicott would pay particular attention to weaning.

In the nursery years, the infant has to contend with the mother's comings and goings: she cannot be ever-present or all-obliging, indeed to be so would hinder development. The tiny child has to realize he can never be fused with her, never return to the womb, nor bask forever, uninterrupted in her arms. (Later analysts, such as the Hungarian émigré to the United States, Margaret Mahler, wrote of the infant's own widening horizons, as it begins to 'toddle', moving exuberantly but also perhaps anxiously from the lap of the mother. This was not just a physical but also a psychical achievement, part of what Mahler called the 'individuation-separation phase'.) Infants may *want* to wriggle free from their mothers' embraces into a wider world, but parents also impose constraints upon the primary wishes to retain an early fusion. The infant realizes that there are rivals for her attention: he or she is not her *only* loved object.

The father not only brings his powerful claim upon the mother but also, as Lacan put it, symbolically says no. Father imposes his name (nom) and 'non' upon the child. He asserts his place with the mother, thus enforcing the taboo upon incest, a regulation that, Freud not unreasonably assumed, exists in all cultures. Whatever Freud ascribed to the paternal function, as many have noted since, this 'third' presence and vital 'no' is not necessarily imposed by an actual father. Evidently we all have a biological father, however remote he may be in our lives; but someone else may represent the third, or it might even be a figure existing inside the primary caregiver's mind.

Recently there has been extensive discussion of the psychological consequences for children of single parents, conceived through new technologies (sometimes with surrogates), or brought up collectively in communes. It can be argued that when the father is not there, an infant might still fashion a paternal figure, as it were, from a friend, relative, or ancestral figure, or indeed from a mother's lesbian partner. Others might question the very idea of calling this position necessarily 'paternal' at all. Yet we must become aware of a point of reference beyond the baby–mother dyad; ultimately of a world, indeed, of relationships *for the mother*. Each of us must recognize here how *she* has a mind, replete with her own longings and losses, and connections to others distinct from our own. A patient of mine once brought a dream in which his mother excitedly rushed up to him and said that she had just seen her own father, out of the blue, bearing cakes and presents. The patient knew that in reality his grandfather had abandoned his daughter (the patient's mother) when she was two, never to return. Part of his work in analysis was to sort out what belonged to whom: where his mother's grief really ended, and where his own began.

In their personal beliefs, analysts cover most of the spectrum of conventional political—and sexual political—views in modern secular societies. They too are influenced by their professional societies, by theory, and by the larger culture. At times some analysts, or analytic institutions, have been cautious or downright reactionary in referring to the life chances of children raised for instance by same sex couples; in other contexts, analysts individually or as a group have been more radical, or strikingly libertarian. Freud himself could be notably relaxed and questioning of social assumptions about sexuality, famously replying to an anxious mother with a homosexual son in a tolerant tone, and with a challenge to the knee-jerk assumption that his orientation was to be regarded as some pathology or defect in itself. Freud's statements on such matters were not always consistent, however.

The key point for Freud was how a paternal figure breaks in upon the nursing couple. He wrote that the superego is heir to the Oedipus complex and retains the character of the father, while the more powerful the Oedipus complex was and the more rapidly it succumbed to repression (under the influence of authority, religious teaching, schooling and reading), the stricter will be the domination of the super-ego over the ego later on—in the form of conscience or perhaps of an unconscious sense of guilt.

The desire to do away with his rival, most notably the father, presents acute problems: it leaves infant and mother alone, but also bereft; it brings fear, and potentially remorse. Freud suggests that the wish for complete union with the mother comes up against the terror of the subject's own annihilation. The infant cannot ignore all of this, cannot 'foreclose' as Lacan later put it, with regard to this paternal (or at least 'third-ness') function, if he or she is to enter the symbolic dimension of language and law, and avoid psychosis: we are obliged to turn elsewhere, realizing that neither mother nor father can be 'ours' in this sense. (Lacan uses a legal term, foreclosure, to suggest a contract that was found to be null to start with, so an Oedipal negotiation was never really made at all.)

Failure to renounce this primary expectation for fusion and possession comes at a heavy cost. Freud set in train a rich seam of inquiries, also pursued by other analysts, into the consequences—when denial, or worse foreclosure, of the Oedipal situation occurs. Freud was particularly interested in the narcissistic blow that all of this brings, as each of us moves from a position as 'his Majesty the Baby', a being for whom practically everything is done, and who may well be treated for a time as the most important person in the world, above all to his mother. To continue to believe ever after, 'l'État, c'est moi' would indeed be delusional.

Gender trouble

The implications of Freud's Oedipal account for theories of homosexuality and for understanding femininity and masculinity have been much debated. Freud, as we have seen, rather privileged the male and heterosexual position. Indeed, even among his followers such assumptions about the consequences of the anatomical differences between the sexes, and the distinct manner in which boys and girls have to deal with their Oedipal problems, were contested. Several women analysts, such as Karen Horney, were among the most vigorous in their challenges to Freud's assumptions.

Freud's accounts suggested the girl has the worse of it, and not only because of cultural norms and prejudices. Some commentators have argued that we should see Freud's presentation as descriptive: charting the mores and neuroses of a particular patriarchal society. Others highlight the way he was prescriptive—suggesting it must always be thus because 'anatomy is destiny'.

Freud believed, controversially, that the infant girl experiences herself as already castrated: her genitals, less visible, are perceived, so he assumed, as lacking her brother's desirable penis. (A crucial point reinforced by Lacan, however, is that the penis, the actual member, is not the 'phallus'; this latter signifies the totemic version of the penis ascribed wondrous powers to restore, complete, and fulfil. Nobody has that magical plenitude. We are all in a state of lack.) Like the boy, the girl must give up her exclusive and all-possessive relationship to the mother; she looks to her father. But then he cannot be hers either; again, like her brother, she has to turn outside the immediate family for another love object. Freud also thought, contentiously, that the girl might seek (in phantasy, via her father) a baby as some compensation for her 'lack' of the penis. He gave less thought to boys' and men's envy of women's capacity to have babies.

Whereas both sexes have to move out, the heterosexual male has switched from one woman to another; the heterosexual woman from mother to father, to another man. Freud believed the girl's (ambivalent) tie to the mother was always, in a sense, more intense and difficult. Her double switch here (of the object and of its gender) was part of the reason why Freud thought sexuality often proved more complicated for girls than boys. Many feminist commentators took issue with Freud's account; some, such as Hélène Cixous, arguing that the girl's marginal position gave her a greater chance of escape from the suffocating 'phallocentric' order. Thus, far more than the boy, the girl might come to enjoy freedom from the superego and the 'paternal law'. Be that as it may, few if any serious clinicians would now hold exactly to Freud's original formulation, in which the girl is simply destined to be the one most prone to bear the envy and suffer the greater sense of lack.

Freud's ideas about Oedipus have continued to resonate in discussions of identity and of sexuality ever since. Lacan's emphasis upon the way we long to discover the desire of the other is also relevant here. A boy or girl, for instance, may want to be a 'real man' or 'authentic woman', but actually be fulfilling what he or she unconsciously imagines to be the unspoken desires of their parents *for him* or *for her*.

Although the boy has an apparently less serpentine route, things soon grow more complicated for him too. Freud presupposes that infant boys and girls alike desire the parent of the same sex, so there is a negative as well as a positive Oedipus complex. Each may wish to merge with, possess, or be possessed by the father *and* the mother. We are all caught, as we work out our Oedipal situation and identifications, between wanting to have and to be, and *not* to have or to be, these primary figures. We have to 'get away', but our difficult struggles amid these early conflicted loves, hates, and fears are likely to resurface sometimes, whatever our age.

A certain style of character may also be used as a disguise, to hide qualities that we imagine others will find unpalatable. Or a persona may be acquired in order, consciously or unconsciously, to curry favour and ward off perceived attack all at once. The analyst Joan Riviere observed this when she suggested how male fears of women, and women's concern about that masculine fear, encouraged a coy and easily accommodating form of femininity; this was a 'masquerade' played out because women suspect that men find their intellectual capacities and strength unwelcome and threatening. Such ideas are relevant in both analytic theory and practice. Our second-guessing about other minds may be well founded, or wide of the mark, but either way it is pertinent in understanding the nature of mind. In analysis, patients may similarly be grappling with the question: what do analysts *really* want, and what can they stand?

Freud's account assumes a kind of rise, fall, and later revival of burning Oedipal feelings. He suggested such preoccupations become more subdued in most children around the age of five or six and then re-emerge with force in puberty, to be reworked as part of the process of adolescence.

The psychological, anthropological, and political implications of Freud's account have been much explored. Historians and social scientists point out that some of the concepts at stake (adolescence, the nuclear family, and so on) are not constant across the ages, nor geographically uniform. The very idea of infancy and childhood is profoundly shaped by culture and place. Nonetheless, it can be argued that the Freudian account of Oedipus, with its focus upon such core triangular relationships in the mind, affords a useful perspective, and one with considerable purchase on psychic truth and people's lived experience. Indeed, whatever the particular familial details, analysts would argue, the Oedipus complex plays a fundamental part in the structuring of the personality.

Chapter 5
Analytic space, time, and technique

A single consultation or few meetings can be valuable, and might even shed helpful new light on a patient's Oedipal or other neurotic problems, but the talking cure typically involves treatment over months, or more likely years, and does not promise change through an epiphany. A patient may have spent years building defences against areas of anxiety and psychic pain; getting past them is not the work of a day. To facilitate analysis, Freud proposed a fixed duration (the session) and a reliable, regular location (the consulting room) ensuring privacy. This chapter explores features of time, space, and distance in this unusual setting, and highlights technique. It is about how analysts work—some dos, don'ts, and divisive experiments.

For instance, it was found best for the analyst not to be entangled in the personal or professional life of the patient, to minimize intrusions, and maintain a set pattern. Freud himself, admittedly, was inconsistent here and conventions grew sharper over the years. Certain patients knew his family. On some occasions he would rather airily discuss theories in the consulting room more in the manner of a teacher. He did not always regard a boundaried setting as crucial, for instance conducting a consultation with the composer Mahler as the two strolled around the Dutch spa town Leyden. More astonishingly, Freud analysed his own daughter, Anna—something that now seems obviously inappropriate.

Klein also dubiously blurred the lines between mother and analyst, deriving and publishing clinical material from her children. Freud warned against conducting 'wild analysis', making speculative deep interpretations of those who are not in treatment (for instance colleagues), even if, admittedly, he was not always himself able to resist. The early followers thought nothing of analysing each other's dreams.

By maintaining firm limits and predictability, we now assume, the analyst is better able to see the patient's shifting attitudes or unconscious reactions to the treatment, and the patient is afforded a consistent 'frame'. The analyst tries to begin and end sessions in a dependable fashion. Even bills are preferably given in the same style each month. Patients react differently to such routines, but also may vary in their own feelings, session by session. A patient of mine unusually failed to produce his cheque one month, said he was baffled, then realized the bill came after a dream about his family; he then remembered what he called an 'explosive thought' he had upon reading the bill: 'If he [the analyst] cared it would cost less, or be free. I bet he asks less from that young woman he sees before me.' This prompted a memory about his suspicion and hurt, as a little boy, that his parents secretly preferred his younger sister.

On time

All kinds of meanings may accrue to the frame; for example, a person may feel it a cruel injustice that the analyst stops promptly on time: 'you should give me five minutes more when I'm really upset', a patient said to me, 'and then shorten the one after if you must...when I'm feeling better'. But complying with this wish would have made it harder to elucidate the feelings stirred up and offered false reassurance. The routine enables the analyst to avoid making omnipotent judgements about whether the work is getting anywhere. A person might unintentionally come early to a session, late to another, and forget a third, and then realize, retrospectively, how this reflects buried feelings of upset about the wait in between. The caricature has it that the analyst automatically presumes that a delay must be of the patient's unconscious making.

A story, probably apocryphal, about Klein concerns a man during the war arriving late for his session after a bomb fell en route; he explained to her the circumstances before adding tartly, 'but I am sure it was my fault'. The point is to be open to the notion that a psychical factor may—*not must*—be in play. Whatever the cause of a delay, the event itself may well generate new meanings and implications in the analysis.

The importance of the reliable, fifty-minute hour has been questioned by some analysts and is not universally applied. Indeed, in the post-war period Lacan's work led to a major row centred upon experiments with variable length sessions, which he justified as a therapeutic tool. The approach meant encounters would end unpredictably (for the patient) when the analyst felt a key moment of psychic significance needed 'punctuating'. Many (myself included) disagree with this approach; it can too easily be capriciously or self-servingly applied, and to my mind adds excessively to an already asymmetrical relationship. It also potentially pits patients against one another; unpunctual endings, after all, might entail uncertain beginnings: a consequence in Lacan's own case, was indeed to have several or even crowds of patients in the waiting room biding their time until their sudden summons, as though courtiers to the King.

Advantages of these added dimensions of uncertainty and interesting clinical uses of the technique and its powerful impact are well described, however, in more down-to-earth language by followers of Lacan such as Bruce Fink. Lacan himself had countered critics by arguing that the predictable analytic hour meant enduring a patient's longwinded diversions on the work of Dostoyevsky, while the variable session unleashed a flood of important, raw material.

Bion on the other hand pointed out that if a patient is proving boring that is really rather an interesting clinical phenomenon in itself, and might better be endured and explored. According to Lacan, however, keeping people on edge in this way could help frustrate the patient's wish for a cosy but useless *tête-a-tête*; analysis, as he once declared, should not be made 'smootchy wootchy'. If such experiments placed him out on a limb, in another sense his adventures in timing were in the bold tradition of Freud, who was alert to the possible value of such shock tactics, conducted, as he put it in the Wolf Man case, absolutely 'in earnest'.

With W it was not a matter of shortening the session, but of abruptly setting a definite termination date without consulting the patient. Freud concluded that W's powerful resistances were leading to stagnation. 'Under the inexorable pressure of this fixed limit,' Freud wrote, 'his resistance and his fixation to the illness gave way, and now in a disproportionately short time the analysis produced all the material which made it possible to clear up his inhibitions and remove his symptoms.' Unfortunately the man's subsequent history gave the lie to any idea that this decision was such a masterstroke.

Nonetheless, the last months in an analysis—when the ending shifts from a vague prospect to a more immediate and real factor—can be especially vivid and moving. Endings may cause patients to communicate with renewed urgency and seek to consolidate rapidly what they have gained; they may also elicit the construction of new defences, or produce a scary feeling of being catapulted back to infancy. There is also some research evidence that the period following termination can prove especially productive, with the analysis still percolating, sometimes most powerfully of all, after it formally ceases.

The kind of ultimatum Freud presented to W is more commonly played out in reverse: patient nonplussing analyst by threatening never to return, or suddenly pulling the plug and calling time.

This takes us back to the early days, when a patient Freud referred to as 'Dora', whom we will encounter again in Chapter 8, walked out on him. Not uncharacteristically, Freud tried to learn from this painful experience.

On the couch

Once underway, analysis typically involves the patient lying down, thereby freed from the analyst's gaze and vice versa. This unusual way of speaking to another person also stems from Freud, and serves, so it is hoped, to facilitate relaxation, enabling the patient's (and analyst's) thoughts to wander freely. Neither party is locked into eye contact, nor having to avoid it. The analyst's attention is, ideally, free-floating rather than primed to look at anything in particular.

Patients have disparate reactions to the couch. Some find reclining initially embarrassing, or even humiliating; others regard it as suggestive, exciting, laid back, or consoling. One patient commented: 'it is like a dentist's chair, only more so'. Another, invited to use the couch, strongly suspected her analyst's power trip, but then said she felt uneasy at being asked to make herself too much 'at home'. 'Do I have to remove my shoes?' Rob asked in his first session before talking of certain fears of contamination. He then opted to sit rather than use the couch, which felt too frightening. A patient who is terrified of a descent into madness may need to see the analyst actually there, distinct from some dreaded or even hallucinated version.

Apparent side reactions about arrangements and even the furniture are not irrelevant: the way a patient personally responds may help bring unconscious thoughts to life. How we enter and leave, perceive the room or the couch, cope with the weekend or a holiday break, deal with time constraints in sessions or the bill, may well be of consequence, even if a new patient might treat such matters as trifling preliminaries to the 'real' business at hand.

Third parties

Analysis, conventionally, requires a discreet setting, a space for the patient to talk confidentially. Thus a third party actually listening in would change conditions markedly. Sometimes recordings have been made for training purposes or in order to conduct trials of different therapeutic methods; however, one should not underestimate (notwithstanding the patient's consent) the potential complications and difficulties. Some would even see this kind of intrusion into standard practice as fundamentally at odds with the essential method, others suggest the most acute discomfort in such circumstances is characteristically the therapist's rather than the patient's, and can be overcome.

Yet even in ordinary analytic treatment, strictly one to one, a patient may talk as though in *implicit* company *beyond* the analyst. We may fear harm to another caused by our words, and, like R, feel terribly overheard or watched. Take the case of a patient who whispers in fear of the indignation a loved one might feel in the face of this 'disloyal' confession. Or perhaps that whispering is to imply, a little seductively, that 'this is for you only...let's keep others out'—something analysts, alert to Oedipal feelings, might well note. Some are consumed by imagining that the analyst is thinking only about their own loved ones; the knowledge that the patient is indeed not, for the analyst, the most important person in the world can be especially painful when the old feelings stirred up are powerful.

Other exceptions exist to this standard one-to-one model; the analytic approach has been applied to the treatment of couples and groups, but again confidentiality is important. Whether an analyst, like a Catholic priest in the confessional, must be bound at all times by the ethic of non-disclosure is a difficult one. Clinicians need regular supervision and a clinical context (seminars and so forth). Freud and his followers also saw the purpose of their work as the pursuit of knowledge of the mind and the furtherance of technique, and so discussed their work and published findings. There is an inevitable conflict here too, between the imperative to disguise the patient's identity fully, and the need to present material faithfully, without too much make-believe.

There are also extreme situations, for example where the clinician might have grounds for fearing for the safety of the patient, his or her dependants, or others, in which it might be essential to talk to a third party to gain advice or avert a calamity. A trend, however, in contemporary society, described by Christopher Bollas and David Sundelson in *The New Informants*, is for therapists of all kinds to be pulled into roles as routine reporters of the patient's progress, or lack thereof, to outside bodies (health insurance companies when paying for treatment, social workers, medical authorities, etc.). This again can create serious conflicts. The danger is that treatment degenerates into analysis by committee, or worse leads to the potential misuse of data for purposes other than therapy.

The debate on such matters continues, since a case can be strongly made for more assessments of 'outcomes', most especially in public health services, so long as safeguards are in place to ensure anonymity and data protection. Certainly there is much about the analytic encounter that is unique and ineffable; it cannot be reduced to number-crunching exercises on 'successes' and 'failures', since the very definition of those terms is so open to question. A personal 'journey of discovery' cannot be 'trialled', as is common for medications.

Yet clearly too, some patients find the process achieves more than others. The psychologist and analyst Peter Fonagy argues that disdain for such testing and/or outside scrutiny has weakened the position of analysis in the public sphere and stems from a complacent form of 'special pleading', the knee-jerk assumption that years on the couch are necessarily the best solution. He points to the growing sophistication of testing methods and shows how trials of psychoanalytical psychotherapy have indeed provided considerable evidence of the method's practical utility, thus bolstering the case for public funding.

Whether or not an analyst is an enthusiast for such trials, or regards them as anathema, he or she requires self-discipline and boundaries—not revealing extraneous information to others, nor about him or herself to the patient, couple, or group in treatment.

Why do analysts need to be patients?

One—undisputed—essential is for analysts to become patients first. The requirement has applied for most of the last century, although in the early days such treatments were often (by modern standards) brief. Personal experience of analysis, admittedly, is no guarantee against subsequent transgressions, but what had already become clear to Freud and his closest lieutenants was that those unanalysed, or only cursorily treated, frequently got into hot water as practitioners for reasons they failed to understand. They *enacted* scenarios, rather than analysing them.

Freud had been faced by the problem of the behaviour of Jung, for example, when he embarked upon an affair with his patient Sabina Spielrein, a debacle later portrayed in a play, in turn made into a feature film, *A Dangerous Method*. The analyst is ethically required to be 'abstinent' in that sense, of course, but also in holding back revelations of personal, undigested emotions about the patient, or others. When working well, the analyst makes use of feelings in formulating an interpretation; that is not the same as confessing one's fantasies, wishes, or dislikes to the patient.

The history of analysis contains some painful as well as shocking examples of practitioners losing their clinical balance in one fashion or another, such is the power of unconscious processes. This is always an occupational risk. Controversy, for instance, surrounds Sándor Ferenczi, Melanie Klein's first analyst, a gifted clinician with an exceptional empathy for human suffering who balked at Freud's rather dispassionate style. For Ferenczi, Freud too easily skirted around the full horror of infantile abuse, including rape. He spelled out the suffering of his patients, but also how he hoped, through his technique, to ameliorate their conditions, through a style much less 'cool' than Freud's. He offered consoling words, self-revelations, and, it would appear, sometimes inappropriate expressions of affection to certain patients, although the exact extent to which he did this remains hotly disputed.

Hearing certain rumours Freud accused him outright of kissing patients, an obvious abuse. Ferenczi in turn sought to reassure Freud, acknowledging in his work and style a certain 'passion', but referring to his 'ascetic' method of 'active therapy'. Much has been written since on his views and actions, and on what may have taken place or been distorted in subsequent, partisan commentaries. Certainly his heartfelt critique of Freud has enduring resonance. But by modifying his analytic approach in the hope of providing a rectifying 'good' experience, Ferenczi understandably caused Freud, and others, disquiet. Accusations that he had simply 'gone mad', however, were overblown; as scholars have shown, these charges against Ferenczi also reflected the complex personal and political tensions of the analytic movement during the 1930s.

Narcissistic blows

The analyst's extended analysis is intended to provide an opportunity to explore unconscious propensities and to work through these, as far as possible, to help the clinician withstand and register pressures coming from the patient, and from within.

The significance of this turnabout in which analyst is first patient was profound, and part of Freud's assault upon human narcissism—not least the narcissism of clinicians. There are always, as Bion puts it, neurotic and psychotic aspects to a personality, albeit not always, of course, in the same proportions.

For Freud, then, the analyst is not 'above' the patient, but someone who has already undertaken a considerable amount of analytic work and other training him or herself. It is one thing for the new trainee to read of neurotic or even quite crazy states in theory, or to witness these in the treatment of others, but quite another to find traces painfully emerging in his or her analysis. That is not to say a moment of madness is the same as full-blown psychosis. Nonetheless, a practitioner who claimed never to have known intense, even mad, jealousy, excessive anxiety, phobias of one kind or another, omnipotent phantasies, envy, murderous thoughts, or melancholy, would be an improbable character and likely a poor analyst of others.

Some therapists prefer to refer to 'clients' in order to reject the medical connotations of the word 'patient', and to make the exchange sound less unequal—the 'client' is the one who might 'hire' or 'fire' the service provider after all. Most psychoanalysts, however, opt for 'analysand', or (as I do here) stick with 'patient', a term at whose root is the idea of a person who is suffering.

Freud thought his work was but the latest in a succession of challenges to human self-love: after the revelations of Copernicus that the sun does not revolve around the earth, and then Darwin's demonstrations of our animal descent and continuing evolutionary state, came Freud's demonstration that not even the ego is master in its own house.

Questions

Ideally, the analyst listens in a state of 'evenly suspended attention'; open to what emerges from the other, and as mindful as possible (paradoxical though this might sound) of unconscious aspects in herself. Questions put by the patient may be left entirely open, or turned into further inquiry. The analyst seeks to explore rather than 'satisfy' such demands. That can be tricky if, for example, the patient is asking whether analysis is useful. Before starting, the analyst might well venture a view. But imagine in the first session a patient asks: 'do any analytic patients ever get well?' Here we would need to pause before rushing in with answers; what instead may be needed is inquiry about what lies behind this question: do *your* patients get well? Will *I* ever get better? Are *you* any good? Am I in safe hands? Can you tolerate my challenging you with this kind of question?

The lack of conventional reassurance ('you will do well') or of 'educational' information ('yes many do get well, here are some articles about psychoanalytic outcomes') might be, for some patients, extremely disconcerting. Yet the very absence of prompts, argument, or polite conversation from the analyst creates a particular opportunity. In the session, the analyst's difficult task is to sustain the role, not become a sparring partner, nurse, teacher, advocate, judge, etc., although often enough we find ourselves unconsciously pulled one way or another to an extent, and then have to recover our function as best we can.

Patients pick up features of their analysts' actual personalities and also distort them. Regardless of how well clinicians maintain their stance, they may find that patients tune in very closely to their private thoughts, or on other occasions treat them as someone or something quite other than they are, as though they have become a reincarnation of a patient's angry father, soothing mother, warring sister, or hectoring spouse. Klein and others showed how the analyst may even be regarded by a patient as a particular aspect of a person or thing, for instance as a generously giving or cruelly depriving breast; she used this rather startling language of body parts very directly, more so indeed than most analysts tend to do today.

Bodies and words

The analyst is trying to attend closely to what the patient says or does. Bodily movements, even certain illnesses, may be invested with meanings which can perhaps reinforce, or run counter to, the ways we overtly do things with words. Bodily actions might also reveal, as Darwin had shown before Freud, traces of our instincts; gestures like scowls and snarls, he had argued, bear evidence of our evolutionary descent. Body–mind relations have been considered in many different medical traditions and systems of thought over the centuries. What Freud offered was a particular way of looking at how certain physical phenomena interact with and express our minds; thus, he explored hysterical uses we can make of the body. In more recent times, the field of psychosomatic conditions has been richly explored by analysts, perhaps most especially in France.

We know that faces or limbs can be made to 'speak', even when a person is silent, and a sluggish or lively walk, dishevelled or immaculate appearance, may be used, consciously or unconsciously, to convey a mental state. Words may be amplified, drained, dramatized, or mocked in their mode of utterance: think for instance how we commonly assume these complexities between the soma and psyche when we combine terms, and talk of how someone is thin or thick skinned, chatters with their hands, gives a tongue lashing, eats humble pie, shakes with rage, bursts with pride, sighs regret, sucks up, is spitting mad, and so on.

Evidently the analyst and patient face choices—such as when and how to speak—albeit not of a precisely symmetrical kind. As in music, silences in the consulting room can be moving, mysterious, pregnant, seductive, defensive, ominous, furious, or suggestive of anxiety. The patient may wrestle with *how* to utter anything, and the analyst may struggle to find an opportune moment to interpret, a time when the patient might actually take the words in.

Endings

Analysis is a transient relationship, although patient and analyst alike may find it difficult to let it go, or even to accept their mortality. How long does the work go on? The analyst should indeed question its excessive continuation, especially if the patient seems to assume its permanence. The trouble is there is no consensus on what 'too long' means. Optimally, there comes a time where analyst and patient resolve the appropriate termination point together, reflecting upon what has been achieved, and what can be realistically tackled: is prolongation a form of addictive dependency (for either or both), or a means of additional, creative endeavour promoting psychic development?

Where analyses in Freud's early days might be over in weeks or months, particular subcultures of analysis developed (worryingly to my mind) to the point where they can endure routinely for many years, with insufficient questioning of the rationale: an assumed way of life, rather than a mode of treatment. This can be exploitative, or even a *folie à deux*. Some patients seem to end up 'nursing' their elderly analysts, who find it hard to retire.

Nonetheless, there are occasions when analysis that persists even for decades may be useful, if it is the choice of a patient who still finds it creative; it may also be the least-worst option for someone otherwise requiring chronic hospitalization. Freud wrote late in his life about the potential interminability of the process, musing on when it might be best to 'let sleeping dogs lie'. Often enough though, patients young or old lack peace of mind; the dogs are not sleeping. That is why patients may be here—or perhaps 'peace of mind' is secured only through a kind of psychic death, cutting the person off from live feeling and contact with others.

Chapter 6
War, politics, and ideas

The debates about technique described in Chapter 5 evolved over decades and owed much to a second generation of clinicians who came to prominence between the 1920s and 1950s. Before considering more closely in Chapter 7 the work of some key figures in that second wave, who have only been mentioned in passing so far, it is important to set the scene and recall the fraught historical context in which psychoanalysis developed. This chapter sketches Freud's later ideas and refers to broader political circumstances prevailing between 1914 and 1945.

Analytic ideas often have two faces: a speculative aspect (so apparent in Freud, who borrowed freely from anthropology, literature, the sciences, or general observations about his family, himself, or the warring world around him), and a more direct clinical component in which unexpected developments with patients lead to new theories.

This is particularly evident in Freud's discussion of the 'death drive', an idea set out in *Beyond the Pleasure Principle* (1920). This variegated work combined grand new theories with observations of Freud's tiny grandson, speculations about biology, reference to myth, and clinical findings in the immediate context of war. Freud suggested how an unconscious force in the psyche could attack the subject's vitality, destroy connections, reduce tensions to the minimum, and aim to restore an inert, even 'inorganic' state. Indeed, he mused about a drive actively working *against* the very will to life. This, it seemed, could be directed inwards, thus facilitating a kind of self-destruction, and could also manifest itself in aggressive and deadly attitudes to others.

The superego, another of his key concepts of this period, could be infused with a merciless and sadistic force, sometimes tearing the subject apart. During and after World War I it was perhaps not surprising that Freud turned to problems of melancholy, death, hatred, and cruelty at the heart of civilization and the mind; he was far from alone in that. At times Freud had tended to imagine (man of his time that he was) what he called 'primitive' people as a separate kind of barbaric entity, at odds with the Europe he knew. Some of his followers spoke blithely and patronizingly of, say, 'the African mind'. Freud also undercut such distinctions, however, seeing the archaic and the irrational as inextricably bound up with the very civilization that he cherished, and, crucially, part of us all. In a famous 1930 book *Civilization and its Discontents*, he amplified his view that we always in part hate the societies and communities that constrain us; while we may value or seek to build them up, another part of us also wants to tear them down.

Freud's early work had laid great stress upon sexuality and its conflicts; his later books and articles during and after World War I gave greater attention to the role of repetition, aggression, and feelings of destructiveness aimed at self, others, or both, and the diverse ways we cope with guilt. In a marvellously suggestive paper in 1917, Freud explored similarities and differences between states of mourning and melancholia. Three years later, in *Beyond the Pleasure Principle*, he also took a fresh look at trauma and the internal sources of insecurity and anxiety, along with his exploration of the death drive. He came to view anxiety not just as a by-product of conflict between the individual's unconscious desire and the dictates of '"civilized" sexual morality'; rather it could be a consequence of a person's own internally torn feelings and thoughts, for instance violent and hate-filled wishes combined with terrifying worries about repercussions. He recognized how the mind could be overwhelmed by both internal and external forces.

In 'Inhibitions, Symptoms and Anxiety' (1926) Freud suggested that anxiety could lead to repression as well as the other way around, with repression evoking subsequent neurotic disquiet. He teased out the difference between fear, where a threat is externally well founded, and neurotic anxiety, a response primarily to threats inside. He was interested too in how forms of panic, redolent of infancy, might return at any stage to flood the subject.

Others took up Freud's ideas about death, aggression, anxiety, and the superego, in accounts of history, politics, and group processes. Nazism, suggested Erich Fromm, was characterized by its craving for endings, deep exultation in suicide and murder, death and deadliness in all its guises.

Opinion has always been divided on the validity of Freud's death drive. Even some analysts have discounted it altogether. Moreover, what orthodox Darwinian could accept the idea of something basic within us all, inimical to the struggle for survival? Yet many clinicians find the concept useful in thinking about lethal and/or totally lethargic states of mind. Freud was also increasingly interested in the relapses suffered by some of his own patients, and the struggles that endure between healthy and ill parts of the self.

Freud and his associates (the majority in his inner circle, fellow Jews) had invented psychoanalysis within the disintegrating world of the Hapsburg Empire. The early analysts had also endured the rise of new populist forms of anti-Semitism in Vienna, shrill nationalism and militarism, and before long industrialized war that led to millions of deaths between 1914 and 1918. In its wake came a terrible flu epidemic (responsible for the death of Freud's own daughter Sophie), years of economic crisis, the rise of fascism, Hitler's seizure of power, ever-intensifying racial persecution, and the breakdown of the fragile international peace.

As Freud lay dying in London in 1939, having escaped Vienna the previous year, a second vast military conflict was in prospect; this he foresaw, but not the full horror of the Holocaust, in which his sisters would perish. From the ruins of war, a new world order emerged after 1945, led by the United States, swiftly shadowed by the prospect of an all-annihilating nuclear exchange. Psychoanalysis was profoundly affected by the century in which it developed, and in turn provided a language that many people thought useful to think about politics and society in the 'age of extremes'.

The International Psychoanalytical Association, founded in 1910, was buffeted by this history. Nonetheless it expanded substantially, gaining increasing influence, especially (between and after the world wars) across the Anglophone world. The movement was never a harmonious band, and differences of opinion proved increasingly stormy before forms of orthodoxy were re-established within new groupings, often based around the ideas and shaped by the personalities of the second generation.

This period of uncertainty and contention, which, in Britain at least, came to a head in World War II, was in part due to the disruption of established societies, and the arrival of analytic refugees seeking homes and livelihoods, and challenging a (precarious) balance. Until 1939 there had been the grand figure of Freud, a participant but also an arbiter in the movement's many disputes. After the founding father's death, competing authorities claimed his mantle, but none had his sway.

Ernest Jones, part of the early circle, became the long-standing president of the British Psychoanalytical Society (established after World War I), and played a major role on the international scene. He was supportive of Klein, who was a radical figure about whom

Freud, and especially his daughter Anna, had serious misgivings. Jones navigated skilfully.

Other once supportive colleagues had long since quit the movement, casting themselves, or cast by others, as renegades. Alfred Adler and Jung had left Freud's circle to found their own separate approaches before 1914. Adler stressed the dynamics of power, and famously introduced the term 'inferiority complex'. He was especially sympathetic to socialism and concerned to foster conditions of greater equality; in fact some of those who remained loyal to Freud also shared these political passions. Jung, particularly interested in mysticism, had become ever more convinced by the idea of collective 'archetypes' playing out in the unconscious, and found Freud's emphasis upon sexuality in neuroses too restrictive.

For different reasons, others, such as Wilhelm Reich, parted company with Freud in the 1930s. Freud was wary of those who rejected his basic theories. Reich's case was both personal and political; Freud certainly had little sympathy with his wish to integrate psychoanalysis and Marxism. Some see the way Freud held the line and ruled the roost as evidence of his unacceptable authoritarianism; others regard it as quite understandable that he guarded his achievements in order to retain the distinctiveness of psychoanalysis as clinical method and theory of the mind.

Hitler's rule caused an exodus of analysts, notably from Berlin, Vienna, and Budapest. The analysts scattered, the largest number going to America. Many contributed to the Allied struggle against the Third Reich. Meanwhile media-savvy popularizers, including Freud's nephew Edward Bernays (an expert in public relations and advertising), championed the unconscious, albeit in simplified form. In the United States ideas such as the Freudian slip and Oedipus complex were embraced by increasing numbers. W.H. Auden (an Englishman who by then resided across the Atlantic) had composed a poem upon Freud's death that included the lines:

'To us he is no more a person | Now but a whole climate of opinion.'
Whether this is an exaggeration depends on whom 'us' refers to:
certainly analysis became increasingly well established in many
metropolitan settings. From its early bases it spread widely; you
could thus find treatment in Edinburgh, Jerusalem, Calcutta, Rio
de Janeiro, Melbourne, Los Angeles, or Johannesburg.

Although analysis was and still is often frequented by
well-educated and relatively affluent people, this is not the whole
picture; many trainees, past and present, have struggled with fees, or
needed financial assistance. Berlin's 'free clinics' in the 1920s were
an expression of the utopian idea of providing analytic therapy for
the 'masses'. The idea that the typical patient or analyst resides
on the Upper West Side in New York or in Hampstead, North
London, is a caricature, even if it serves to point up how analysts
often cluster into small communities, and how availability of
treatment is anything but uniform.

Analysis, however, has always been far more than a private form
of practice; it spread into public health services and also into
experimental treatment centres run by a few sympathetic military
psychiatrists for so-called shell-shocked soldiers or, later, 'war
neurotics' The ideal of one-to-one treatment for large numbers
waxed and waned across the 20th century. Only a minority even of
middle-class populations ever underwent full-blown analysis even
at its high water mark in wider culture.

Nonetheless, a good number of people without the means of
standard treatment have long found vacancies at low if any cost
through training schemes run by the major institutes, such as in
London. In certain parts of the UK, in economically buoyant
times, it has been possible to have psychoanalytical psychotherapy
on the National Health Service, albeit usually only for a strictly
limited duration. In the current climate, even that option is
severely eroded. In Germany it has often proved feasible for
patients to have the talking cure supported by health insurance.

Analysis, interwar and post-war, remained a ferment of ideas; aspects of its theories were put to use, for example, in experimental schools, projects for 'juvenile delinquents', and children's wards. It was once commonplace to insist that parents should not stay with their children in hospital, since 'it would only upset them'. The analysts John Bowlby and René Spitz led the charge against such timeworn assumptions, respectively, in Britain and America. A 1952 film inspired by such work by James Robertson, *A Two-Year-Old Goes to Hospital*, demonstrated more powerfully than any dry report the case for reform. What various observational studies revealed was that children abruptly separated from parents might well be in a state of listless despair, rather than stoical acceptance of their lot.

The analytic focus upon early nurture and mothering struck a chord after 1945, resonating with welfare policies that aspired to provide 'cradle to grave' care. Bowlby influentially warned of the damaging consequences of prematurely broken bonds, above all between infant and mother. A branch of the discipline, now known as attachment theory, was inspired by his work. Bowlby's targets included the English public school boarding system, where the sons of the socially privileged were often sent away aged seven—a practice he regarded as an abomination, having experienced it himself.

One of the key developments of the 1940s was analytic group work, thanks to the pioneering experimentation of S.H. Foulkes, Bion, and others. This also chimed in with political aspirations to foster more egalitarian social structures, encourage new forms of social collaboration, and tolerate interpersonal differences. The rise of group analysis went together with projects to make 'therapeutic communities' for the mentally ill, rejecting an old 'top down' management of the old asylums. Some analysts were actively engaged in applying Freudian methods in international initiatives, for example regarding selection and recruitment to civil service and army posts in occupied Germany, contributing to the attempt to weed out the most dangerous 'authoritarian types'.

If Freudian thought attracted devotees from most of the political range, its ethos was essentially anti-totalitarian. Freud's books were burned in Germany after the Nazis came to power in 1933. A bizarre version of psychotherapy endured in the Third Reich. Known as the Göring Institute, a revamped Berlin psychotherapy centre paid homage to Hitler and relied on a medley of theories of racial difference, mental hygiene, and the unconscious. Psychoanalysis itself was well tolerated in certain authoritarian, military regimes in post-war Latin America. There were even some notorious cases of analysts collaborating with the security apparatus in such states, but most kept their heads down, working on as before or fleeing, while others actively joined in the resistance.

The radicalism of Freud's *psychological* account led some to view analysis as a natural bedfellow for *political* revolution on the left. Yet camp followers of the psychoanalytic movement included many liberals and social democrats, and also, perhaps more surprisingly, some influential neo-conservative thinkers in America, seeing in Freud's 'tragic vision of man' and jaundiced view of 'the masses' justification for scepticism about egalitarian change. The counter-culture of the 1960s saw new attempts (following earlier endeavours by 'left wing Freudians' during the interwar period) to marry a theory of the unconscious to Marxism.

In Stalin's Russia and Mao's China, by contrast, it was impossible for psychoanalysis to thrive. Interest in Freud, once shown by Trotsky, increasingly went underground following his departure from the scene in the 1920s; the orthodox view mostly prevailed that the psychoanalyst was an incorrigibly bourgeois figure, of no relevance in a communist society. More recently analysis has found a new purchase in these countries, as it has also done in some other parts of the former Eastern bloc.

Freud or Marx? Writers such as Fromm worried away at the question. For some there seemed to be a requirement to make an absolute choice, but others—notably a group of researchers forced into exile in the United States, collectively known as 'the Frankfurt School' and who temporarily counted Fromm in their ranks—pioneered social theories that combined elements of both.

It is commonplace for critics to claim that analysis is a means of depoliticizing people, focusing on individual pain rather than family dynamics, still less collective social injustices. This no doubt can be the case, most obviously if the analyst colludes in a patient's narcissistic phantasy that the self is all that matters. Yet it surely need not be so; for it is also true that analysis might invite greater curiosity about the *relationship* between avowed politics and unconscious wishes. It has, for instance, been of great importance in exploring more deeply the appeal of racist beliefs. It might help us to see how politics mobilizes phantasies or relies upon projections, even as it concerns material struggles and competing social interests.

Analysis is not necessarily about making people more accepting of and resigned to how the home or the world is, although admittedly schools such as the ego psychologists sometime encouraged, too unquestioningly, an 'accommodation' with society in the name of mental health. Analysis might well *not* lead a patient to become more resigned, still less more passive; it might also allow somebody to get in touch with anger, to look for more far-reaching solutions to problems, and to work more effectively with others. And it might elicit the patient's curiosity about why change is so difficult and what transformations, personal or social, may yet be possible.

Marie Langer, an analyst and communist supporter who fled Austria for Uruguay and soon after Argentina, challenged any notion that psychoanalysts should stay out of politics. She criticized governments and analysts who collaborated with them, and was obliged to leave Argentina and flee to Mexico in the 1970s when threatened with arrest. She developed close links with liberation movements, and denounced the authoritarianism she witnessed in several of the South American analytic institutes. In a different context, in Britain in 1987, the analyst and socialist Hanna Segal published an influential paper about the nuclear arms race, entitled 'Silence is the real crime'. Practitioners like her engaged quite prominently in politics of one kind or another.

During the second half of the 20th century analytic approaches ramified, so it may make more sense now to talk of *psychoanalyses* rather than to imagine a single, even notionally unified field. Influential interpreters and innovators—such as Lacan in France, Klein, Bion, and Winnicott in Britain, and Hartmann in America—certainly gave the field their own particular stamp. It was to prove increasingly hard, or in some cases impossible, to claim that these individuals, or many others who experimented with technique in the tracks of Freud, were all 'on the same page'. Chapter 7 looks in more detail at affinities and differences between some of the key analytic approaches to emerge post-war, especially in America, France, and Britain.

Chapter 7
Further innovations and controversies

In an interview in 1990, Laplanche protested against the 'social adaptation of the profession'. He sharply criticized those seeking to impose upon analysis 'any pre-established social aim', arguing that the treatment 'is purely a personal question'. He rejected the distinction between clinical and theoretical matters, questioning the privileged category of training analysts (those selected by their organizations in order to analyse would-be analysts), and any assumption that the field itself belongs to the formal analytical societies anyway.

'This is very radical', murmured his interviewer. Yes, said Laplanche, adding that he expected such radicalism to be defeated, given the 'social pressure to prescribe all forms of human activity'. Laplanche had established a distance from his analyst and colleague, Lacan, many years earlier, following disagreements over theory and technique. Laplanche's combative position was in tune, however, with a tradition within French analysis, substantially inspired by Lacan: this was a battle against the perceived 'normalization' of Freudian thought, bureaucratization of organizations, and instrumental use of analysis to adapt the subject to the prevailing political order.

Ego psychology

A tradition that became prominent in post-war America, 'ego psychology', was an old and obvious target for the kind of criticisms by Laplanche just described. This was a wing of the movement led by Heinz Hartmann, Ernst Kris, and others, which prospered, post-war, in the United States. Among Hartmann's collaborators was Lacan's one-time analyst, Rudolph Loewenstein. The group were based in New York, following their flight from Nazi-occupied Europe.

While these analysts did much to consolidate the status of the talking cure, this achievement came at a price. Certainly many, including Lacan, balked at their vision of analysis facilitating a 'healthy' ego's optimal adaptation, fine-tuned to test reality, albeit allowing some margin for individual compulsions, idiosyncrasies, and passions. Lacan saw ego psychology as itself an adaptation of Freud's ideas to an individualistic, optimistic society, replete with rose-tinted dreams. Ego psychology led to challenges from within American analysis too. Indeed, many clinicians who became influential in subsequent decades, such as Heinz Kohut, Otto Kernberg, Roy Schaffer, or Stephen Mitchell, established their positions in contradistinction to ideas once advanced by Hartmann and his group, just as, in France, Lacan was a stimulant for subsequent developments by both supporters and opponents.

In one sense, the ego psychologists had taken their lead from Freud, but tended to simplify his account, viewing too complacently the well-functioning ego as the rational organ of mind; when well-analysed, the ego as Hartmann saw it for example, could apparently operate mostly conflict-free and, at least potentially, uncontaminated by the unconscious. He and the other ego psychologists also especially lauded the work of Anna Freud, who had produced an important book in 1936 on the ego and its defences.

The task for Hartmann (as Schaffer has put it) was to enhance the patient's capacity to engage in 'rational action and...stable object relations', and to exercise 'dispassionate judgment'. Although well versed in analytic theory, Hartmann set much less store by Freud's depiction of the ego as necessarily divided within itself, and always partly *unconscious*. This unconscious dimension was apparent, Freud had claimed, in the way the ego might be busy repressing unwelcome thoughts without the person concerned being any the wiser that this was happening at all.

The ego is a malleable concept; in everyday speech people might use it almost as a synonym for 'me' or the essential, unadulterated self. Lacan, among others, begged to differ. Freud had also already shown how the ego is formed from a composite of images, emotional ties, and identifications with others. Evidently Freud's own remarks invite competing visions; many other analysts used those American interpretations of Freudian thought as a spur, arguing in opposition to Hartmann and his circle that the ego is the place in which we might be most inclined to misperceive ourselves; the aim of analysis, it was argued, is not to reinforce the illusions of ego, but to investigate the constructions of our subjectivity.

Critics have also complained that the ego psychologists oversimplified the nature of work with patients, casting the analyst as (to borrow Schaffer's words again) a potentially 'reasonably objective observer' of the session, 'a non-participant in the observational field of clinical practice', who accordingly could 'take an absolute stand on what is going on in that field'.

Hartmann was especially keen to reconcile analysis with the findings of biology, and stressed the organism's *natural* need to fit in with its environment. In this and other propositions, in fact, there was dissension even within his circle, and among those he influenced: another indication that generalizations about what entire 'schools' of analysis claim or believe can be quite misleading.

Lacan

Lacan's talent and ambition within the analytic movement were
signalled in the 1930s and became more fully apparent post-war.
Orthodox enough an analytic candidate (he trained as a doctor
and psychiatrist first), he was, however, unusually steeped in
philosophy, including Hegel and Heidegger. Intrigued by
surrealism, Lacan had known many of the Parisian avant-garde.
Apparently, he had even heard James Joyce reading his work at
the Shakespeare and Company Bookshop in the French capital in
1921. Lacan had a considerable gift, perhaps in part inspired by
Joyce, for bending words into witty and telling new combinations.
This capacity demonstrated, in accordance with Freud too, how
meanings are multifarious.

Lacan read Freud through the prism of several modern human
sciences, including structural anthropology and the linguistic
theories of Saussure. The latter had set out a theory of signs, based
on the distinction between 'signifiers' and 'signifieds'. One signifier,
for instance 'drone', can have many signifieds (such as 'speak low
and boringly', 'male bee', or 'pilotless aircraft'); and of course we all
have our own associations to each of these possible signifieds.

Desire too, Lacan claimed in his own erudite and tantalizing
style, is always *in excess*, impossible to pin down or limit to the
ostensible thing we require. Even as demands are articulated
and sometimes met, desire slips through—beyond any kind of
possible, complete satisfaction. We may long nonetheless for some
final resolution of our desires, or for plenitude. Lacan described in
various ways how we are bound up with our own images, in a
dyadic bond with mother, caught up in a hall of mirrors, involving,
perhaps, dreamy visions of fusion, a state of affairs to which he
gave elaborate attention and termed 'the imaginary'.

But his work was a moving target. He established the contrast, for
example, between those psychical orders that he named 'the

imaginary', 'the symbolic' (the shared realm of language and law that is ushered in, crucially as we saw in Chapter 4, through the paternal figure who interrupts the one-to-one relationship between infant and mother), and 'the real'. But no sooner had he done so, than he complicated his account, showing the degree to which these concepts overlapped with and were bound up, inextricably, with each other.

For Lacan we exist in a state of lack, caught in languages that are never, primarily, of our own making—subjects within an endless 'signifying chain' that is there before we are born and there after we die. Words always lead on to more, as we know when we look them up in a dictionary. And yet, Lacan argued, we continue on our quests for the centre and the last word, in search of some Wizard of Oz perhaps—a presumed authority, or what Lacan called 'a subject supposed to know'.

But neither the essential fractures in our being, nor the endless circuit of desire, can really be brought to a close. Lacan showed how a particular person's desire interacts with, indeed requires, another's: so we desire to locate the desire of the other, searching out, for example, what it is that a parent, lover, child, or analyst really seeks in us, just as those others do with their others, ad infinitum. We are creatures endeavouring not only to gain recognition or satisfaction from the other, but also to figure out, ultimately, what is wanted from us.

The patient, Lacan found, often turns to the analyst to provide a coveted 'imaginary' form of support, as though mirroring or completing us. He noted how patients might demand that the analyst should be the all-knowing subject, and fill in the fractures. But the analyst's role is to confront the subject with their desire, not falsely to reassure. Analysts who follow Lacan aim always to spur on the patient's capacity to free associate, rather than to 'satisfy' illusory wishes. This is no monopoly of Lacanian practitioners, but they lay particular stress on sustaining the enigmatic and non-compliant aspect of the analyst's role.

Lacan offered a striking new vision of the predicaments of being human, and in his grand claims he became a key figure to argue with, thus attracting critical responses not only from other analysts, but also from philosophical luminaries such as Jacques Derrida. A number of influential writers who have explored sexuality, gender, and the psychic lives of women, such as Luce Irigaray and Julia Kristeva, also found Lacan an indispensable reference point, even as they came to challenge some of his claims. In fact, none of the most significant writers in the psychoanalytic field to emerge in France such as Laplanche or André Green can be understood without reference to Lacan.

The early and now much celebrated paper on the 'mirror phase' in 1936 was but the first of Lacan's many key interventions, suggesting that the ego is constituted in a most peculiar way through our relationship to our own images. He showed time and time again how we might see and identify with the reflection, egged on by another onlooker, most obviously the mother. He drew attention to this critical guiding role of another in constituting our egos: for instance the parent who says excitedly, 'look there you are!' as the little one peers into the mirror and jubilantly starts to regard its previously uncoordinated body and mind as some kind of unity, discrete unto itself.

Lacan's ideas ramified and, not surprisingly given their often fiendishly complex formulation, caused much puzzlement. Some concluded that his copious discourses had pearls of wisdom as well as much dross. Others became zealous devotees, or, by contrast, rejected him as a provocative charlatan. His influence derived in substantial part from his live presentations. There was an irony in the adulation, given his insistence on the illusions of mastery, but for some his disclaimers only added to his allure. Great crowds would flock to his seminars, initiated in the 1950s. Lacan was suspicious of the way analytic ideas could become petrified in print, and enjoyed a formidable capacity to improvise, although in fact now much of his work is published. His thought remains influential in numerous clinical groups and humanities departments in universities across the world. It has been given great prominence more recently by the prolific cultural critic, political activist, and philosopher, Slavoj Žižek.

Žižek has made much of 'the real', a concept first mooted by Lacan in the 1930s and developed post-war. Quite distinct from Freud's description of 'the reality principle', Lacan meant that which falls outside the symbolic—beyond all language, law, and representation; a presence we might glimpse in certain traumatic moments when symbolic systems founder or disintegrate. Some apparently felt, for example, when witnessing the Twin Towers collapse on 9/11, as though *everything* was coming apart, this event being a horror beyond all others.

Lacan's 'real' refers to something potentially terrifying and outside comprehension: 'the real is that which resists symbolisation absolutely', he wrote. Žižek has tried to portray this through horror movies in which we sense 'the primordial abyss that swallows everything', 'dissolving all identities'. He pointed to *Alien*, directed by Ridley Scott and set in distant space, suggesting that the film stages a momentarily incomprehensible 'real' moment when we, as viewers and even the onlookers within the film, stare on aghast as a monstrous, live creature breaks out from within the chest of a writhing man. Legend has it that in order to capture their stupefaction all the more the other actors were not told what would happen. There is a paradox here, as Žižek is aware: as soon as the 'real' is envisaged (for instance caught *in* a moment of film) it disappears, no longer outside representation. It is hard to depict 'the real' as something truly ungraspable, without simultaneously dispelling it. But there are, as he puts it, certain images that 'endeavor to stretch the imagination to the very border of the unrepresentable'.

Klein

Klein, too, was to gather admirers but also be much criticized for erring from the 'correct' Freudian path. Yet she saw her theories as a loyal development of Freud's. Although her work was sometimes pilloried or ignored (it gained little traction for many years in the United States, for example), Klein had a major impact on her colleagues in Britain and then internationally.

Born in Vienna, she lived in Budapest, then Berlin, before settling permanently in London during the 1920s. Some there expressed a touch of condescension (finding her too strident or a bit gauche), while admiring her nonetheless for her courage and clarity. Among those to encounter her and comment on her work and character were various members of the celebrated 'Bloomsbury' group, which included Virginia and Leonard Woolf and the analyst James Strachey (who made important analytic contributions in his own right).

Klein did not have Freud's great knack for writing, but produced landmark papers and books documenting her profound, path-breaking work with children and advancing several new remarkable concepts for understanding the mind. With the arrival of various exiles from Nazi Europe during the following decade, including Sigmund and Anna Freud in 1938, the British Psychoanalytical Society was faced with a sharpening divide. Among the most acrimonious and in the end implacable criticisms Klein received were those of Melitta Schmideberg, her own daughter and herself an analyst. They were never reconciled.

Different views, seasoned by intense personality clashes, culminated during World War II in what became known as the 'controversial discussions' at the British Psychoanalytical Society. Klein's work was a major factor in these polemics about theory, technique, and teaching; among her most powerful opponents was Anna Freud, who believed Klein had moved too far away from her father's and her own ideas. Nonetheless, in the end compromise was reached—a so-called 'gentleman's agreement' to share in the ownership, training programme, and future direction of the Society.

Both women treated children but had strikingly different ideas about how that work should be conducted. Children, as we saw in Chapter 1, would be offered play materials to enable free expression. The analyst would observe closely how the child played with the 'little wooden men and women, carts, carriages, motor-cars, trains, animals, bricks and houses' provided, or used the paper, scissors, and pencils, then make interpretations.

Some critics suggested that Klein might be reading too much into the material, or even declaring to the little patient that she had found *in them* the very things she was looking for. But she was unfazed, continuing to illustrate infantile preoccupations with sexuality and the primal scene, as well as with states of aggression and destructiveness; she showed the way her patients' moods might oscillate between adoration, detestation, and terror of the most vicious retaliation; and she described how each might also seek to make reparation and reconstitute a 'good object' that had been temporarily lost or broken up in their own minds.

Klein rejected Anna Freud's view that the analyst might need to have 'educational' aims, especially at the start. Anna also thought the transference factor in child analysis might be less evident than with adult patients, since their dominant, live relationship was to the parents. Klein sought to identify and speak outright with the child about his or her deepest anxieties whenever she could find them. Such frank interpretation, she believed, offered truer support than conventionally consoling words. You can see in Klein's writings how tenaciously she approached the task of exploring patients' raw and terrifying feelings of love, hate, envy, loneliness, or helpless anxiety. Some of her later followers, such as Betty Joseph, pursued still further, in fine grain, this idea of the 'total transference' situation, considering how *all* that is said and done (each specific response by a patient to an interpretation for example) may be used to explore potential unconscious meaning.

At the centre of analytic inquiry, for Klein, was always the constantly *relational* dimension of mind. Just as patient and analyst interact, so the ego is also relating to itself and others. For her the key word here was 'objects'. Once again Freud was the inspiration: during the 1910s and 1920s he had paid more attention to the constant traffic within the mind—between the ego and itself, and between the ego and other forces. He had shown how the ego could become split into a subject and object part. So in states of narcissism, for instance, we are divided into a viewer and a viewed, and can look on adoringly at self-reflections.

Klein and others, such as a colleague in Scotland called Ronald Fairbairn, took up that crucial relational idea, exploring the ways we might torment, fight, or make peace with our egos, and with various different kinds of internal objects. They argued that from earliest infancy we are caught up in emotionally charged and consequential internal as well as external relationships. Klein went still further, suggesting how the patient (adult or child) might be dealing in phantasy with component parts of a person as though a live creature in itself: a nipple, vagina, or penis, a tummy, mouth, or anus may themselves be perceived as animate and 'minded'—desiring, punishing, controlling, depriving, tormenting, healing, or loving in their own right.

In 1926 Klein wrote: 'at a very early age children become acquainted with reality through the deprivations it imposes on them. They defend themselves against reality by repudiating it.' But the fundamental thing, the criterion of capacity for successful coping with reality, is the degree to which 'they are able to tolerate the deprivations that result from the Oedipal situation'. She pushed back the timeline of the Oedipus complex to the first two years of life, and linked this struggle with a concept that she called the 'depressive position'.

As Klein explained in 1935, the depressive position is marked by a person's enhanced capacity to bring things together, tolerate mixed feelings towards the self and others, and bear exclusion and loss. In the depressive position, we are more able to mourn the damage we do in our phantasies (or sometimes too in actuality), and realize we are not in fact all-powerful in controlling or reconstituting others at will. We are, crucially, *concerned* here for the object. In this state we have a wish to repair our destructive impulses and effects and are more cognizant of our guilt and limitations. It is important to note that by depressive position she did not mean the same thing as 'melancholia'; nonetheless we might well feel, in this state, a tinge (or more) of sadness, and are faced by a work of mourning.

Klein talked of 'positions', not 'stages'. We oscillate between this more integrated ('depressive') position and another condition of mind, more obviously marked by paranoid fears of attack upon ourselves and a process of splitting. In this condition, associated with the earliest, least-integrated emotions, the dominant anxiety concerns survival, and we protect our fragile psyche through mechanisms to keep what seems 'good' or 'bad' utterly apart. She called this fragmented and persecutory state of affairs the paranoid schizoid position, and regarded the attainment of the depressive position as a key developmental achievement that is reached, then lost and regained over and over again. These oscillations are evident when we are plunged back into more persecuted, frantic, and fragmented states, for instance at times of vulnerability and stress.

Winnicott

Each of the main figures discussed in this chapter was both an inspiration to others and a catalyst for argument and new approaches. This was clearly the case for the English paediatrician and analyst Winnicott, who admired but also criticized Klein, pursuing an original line of thought in a strikingly accessible style.

He placed greater emphasis upon actual parents and their role in shaping the infant's mind. Winnicott observed many mothers and babies close up, and built his observations into a working theory. He famously postulated that a 'good enough mother' is one who functions for a time with an extra-acute sensitivity, but does not presume to be perfect, indeed who necessarily must dis-illusion the infant. She is able, gradually, to let go. The capacity for acute tuning in, he suggested, is especially evident in most mothers quite spontaneously, during the later stages of pregnancy, until weeks or months after birth. He called this a state of 'primary maternal preoccupation'. We rely upon this nurture in order to thrive, and gather up enough identity to become a real person, truly psychically alive.

In 'good enough' experience, the mother gradually starts to reclaim her body and mind, and to open up space for the child's own movement away from her; mother and baby do not remain glued together indefinitely, and the infant finds various means of moving out of this dyad, for instance via heavily invested toys or a comforting scarf of the mother's, perhaps still retaining something of her scent. Winnicott referred to such treasured possessions as 'transitional objects'.

Winnicott gave much thought to the role of play in early life, and after. This too built on work by Freud, who had written a remarkable account of an infant's attempt, through a game, to cope with his mother's departure in *Beyond the Pleasure Principle*. Freud had observed the tiny boy, in fact his grandson, repeatedly throwing away and then retrieving a cotton reel. Freud regarded the reel as a symbol of the absent mother, observing that the game followed swiftly on her departure. If it enabled him to achieve a grasp, even a sense of mastery, over an occurrence that he could not in reality dictate, Freud was nevertheless struck at how insistently he kept staging the loss.

Too much deprivation—for instance the long-term absence of loving care—and other violent impingements on early experience, might lead an infant to adapt to the environment by way of a 'False Self', Winnicott argued. He recognized as inevitable that mothers would at time feel hatred as well as love for their babies and children; it was always a question of degree and duration. He showed how too much deprivation or pressure to comply with the caregiver could be calamitous to the fragile early self. It made no sense to talk of a baby (or for that matter of anyone at all) as a discrete, self-sufficient individual. His descriptions of babies, their parents, and why all of this early interaction mattered so much to subsequent mental health, were aired in his popular books and in BBC radio broadcasts.

Where some critics suggested Freud focused on the paternal function to excess, others accused Winnicott and Bowlby of giving too much emphasis to the formative influence (and responsibility) of the mother and her milieu. The importance of this 'facilitating', especially maternal, environment did not necessarily imply women are culpable in returning to work outside the home, but many felt burdened, as well as liberated, by such messages. These analysts' insights could certainly be given both a progressive or reactionary gloss.

Bion

Bion, an important theorist, analyst, teacher, and writer, was inspired by Klein as well as Freud, and became an influential figure, teaching in Britain then on the Continent and the Americas (he emigrated from London to Los Angeles late in his life). Bion's writings cover a very wide range, and include fascinating reflections on his own early life, including his experiences in the army, as a tank commander in France during World War I. As supervisor and teacher, he was noted for his terse formulations and pithy comments—on one occasion he is said to have remarked to an overconfident colleague presenting work in a seminar, 'I think the patient is trying to tell you he thinks you are a bloody fool'.

Bion also offered memorable clinical descriptions, especially of work with psychotic patients. He wrote of a man who appeared to mirror his analyst's every gesture before lying on the couch, 'as if we were both parts of the same clockwork toy'. That patient was apparently hallucinating as he lay down, gazed at the floor, then shuddered almost imperceptibly. Minutely recording such gestures, Bion provided the reader with a vivid sense of the atmosphere, and of the patient's emptiness, anxiety, and incapacity. Bion also noted how the patient used his eyes as though they were devouring and expulsive organs rather than a means of sight. He had an acute awareness of the multiple meanings (as he put it) that 'verbs of sense' have for us all, but especially for the psychotic, and he managed to talk with severely ill patients about the way seeing and other senses may be experienced in the most bizarre ways.

Bion described how a particular, disturbed patient might regard things in the consulting room as composed of extremely hostile elements. Such objects, which may appear innocuous to the bystander, contain the extruded contents of the patient's own smashed up and then emptied-out mind. The analyst's first task here, he wants to show us, is to make no presupposition in advance, thus to try to gain a proper, accurate sense of what it is the patient in question actually 'sees' or 'hears', however mad. One of Bion's many memorable remarks was a suggestion that the analyst try to approach the session without 'memory or desire'.

Bion was especially interested in what is meant by thinking and what function it serves. A process of thinking, he argued, emerges (or sometimes fails to) in order to deal with thoughts. The latter after all can erupt violently like internal missiles—explosive, unexpected, and potentially unbearable, in infancy and throughout life—so we need some means of coping with and constraining them, and at times we all try desperately to get rid of them.

Bion was also a pioneer of group work. He was equally alert to how individuals and groups deal with, avoid, or entirely ignore awkward and unwelcome information that emerges, build more complex conceptual structures, or attack the very possibility of linking thoughts at all. He asked what equips us, alone or *en masse*, to digest and learn from experience, become ever more deadened, or whipped up and shrill, blind to reality.

His depiction of what he called 'the work group' that engages in creative and (sometimes) painful thinking is an antidote to an earlier crowd psychology that treated human aggregates as almost bound to descend into 'primitive' and violent states. He differentiated 'work groups' from 'basic assumption' groups; the latter dominated by powerful unexamined (unconscious) beliefs. Alone or together our capacities to think and to manage thoughts and feelings are precarious psychic achievements.

Affinities

Bion, like Winnicott, theorized the function of the mother/carer in facilitating and sustaining psychic growth, describing the importance of one mind for another throughout life. He wrote of the importance of the 'container', exploring the function that the other's mind holds, above all for the infant's. Feelings become more tolerable and amenable to understanding, via the containing function of the primary carer. If all goes well, this gradually comes to be internalized, so that (up to a point) we can 'contain' and 'digest' our moments of frustration, disappointment, or even blind rage.

Bion made extensive use of an idea of Klein's called 'projective identification'. This referred to a mechanism we all use unconsciously to some degree, in order to try to eject qualities of ourselves (feelings, capacities) into another's mind, so that this other takes on something of our own hue. If this process can relieve us of something intolerable it may also serve, Bion suggested, to communicate unconsciously what it feels like inside, thus enabling another to register this state and react helpfully.

Good things as well as bad may be 'put into' others. I may wish, for instance, to be rid of a nasty mood and dump it with another person, who then carries a portion of 'me'. If successful, my irritation or rage effectively gets under someone else's skin (a parent's, or an analyst's, for example). Having done this, I might feel a bit better, albeit hollowed out; it is equally possible unconsciously to imagine that the other is 'in a state', when in fact they are not particularly disturbed. A mother for instance may be driven frantic by a baby, just as an analyst may sometimes be made desperate by a patient, but a mother may also contain the baby's frantic effort to expel its own feelings without being overwhelmed herself.

Bion's account of mental mechanisms, like Winnicott's, has proved enormously suggestive in thinking about mother–infant interactions as prototypes of all others, and locating echoes of these raw states and containing functions within clinical work. He saw the mother as a crucial psychic repository, helping by taking in from her baby the most difficult feelings, digesting, modifying, and responding in a way that can be used to cope with an otherwise intolerable mood, then giving something back to the baby through further interaction.

So while these analytic writers pursued different lines, there were also certain affinities. Lacan and Klein were concerned, albeit in quite different fashions, to get back to what was most truly disturbing and innovative in Freud's ideas about the unconscious. Like Winnicott, Bion stressed the vital role in psychic life of a receptive and attuned caregiver, and examined how we process (or fail to) the myriad thoughts and feelings that impinge within our minds. Both talked of certain overwhelming psychic experiences as akin to terrible falls into the void or nameless feelings of dread.

Winnicott shared with Lacan a particular fascination with the meanings of mirroring. Lacan and Bion were both attracted, for better or for worse, to the economy of algebraic formulations. Bion described the will to knowledge as 'K'. He built here on Klein who talked of an instinctual desire to know and to explore, which she had called an epistemophilic impulse. Bion was no less interested in the forces inside that may sabotage and destroy that impulse, dismantling the very tools of mind and psychic connections that enable 'K' to be pursued. This force he called simply 'minus K'. There are parallels here too with Lacan, who posited a certain human passion for ignorance.

Schools of thought

Distinct approaches within psychoanalysis owe much to individual clinicians such as those already described; they also reflect wider differences in national culture and thought, as can be seen in the various micro-histories of the movement that have been written, ranging from Argentina and Australia, to India and Italy, and from Britain to Russia, or from France to the United States.

Each national context has been decidedly different, and there have also been notable variations in training and technique, despite some past attempts to standardize procedures. Many French analysts, whose practice has been shaped by Lacan, tend to regard their British counterparts (many of whom have been rather more influenced by Klein) as prone to interrupt excessively, overdo their interpretations, and be too emphatic. The latter are quite likely to wonder why many of their Gallic colleagues are quite so reticent and ambiguous, and in turn make a case that it is better to speak out plainly, and be less theoretical and more 'empirical'. Caricature of psychoanalytic cultures, nations, and schools, however, is all too easy! Many of these distinctions and disputes have been just as apparent *within* particular analytical organizations, or even groupings, as they have been markers of international antagonisms.

In the United States in recent years, there has been an upsurge of work considering the two-way nature of the analytic process.

A number of influential clinicians, such as the late Stephen Mitchell, explored concepts such as 'inter-subjectivity', itself now the catalyst for several schools of thought. Such work shows how wide is the spectrum of views about what and how much the analyst might usefully say, and what he or she intentionally as well as unintentionally might reveal to the patient.

In my view the analytic stance does involve, crucially, an exploration of human interaction, but it also requires the kind of 'abstinence' in the analyst that I describe in Chapter 6. This is not silence in the manner of a Trappist monk, nor is it a claim to a state of impersonality, or to achieve ultimate neutrality, still less a state of unruffled objectivity.

But it is not enough for the analyst just to create the analytic space and then withdraw, nor is it appropriate for the analyst garrulously to 'emote'. To enter into what has been called 'mutual analysis' is highly problematic. This particular approach has several sources, but can be traced back to experiments among Freud's early followers about how to help patients the most, notably provoked by Ferenczi during the interwar period. He had increasingly doubted, as we have already seen, that 'holding back' in the manner advised by Freud was therapeutically helpful. An emotionally corrective experience of warmth, he believed, might be necessary for patients who had suffered deprivation or trauma. While he made an important point about the power of trauma, and the risks of classical analysis itself being unbearable to some patients, the idea of the therapist providing a compensatory experience is questionable too, and may well leave the patient less if any room to expose their own negative or hostile feelings to the analyst.

While most, perhaps even all, analysts would now agree that both parties affect each other unconsciously, some now go further, suggesting free associations should flow both ways; the analyst perhaps proffering dreams, memories, or private associations as well, when deemed relevant, i.e. as stirred by the patient. At worst, this approach has substituted an equally dubious 'let it all hang out' alternative in place of the more forbidding and sometimes excessively withdrawn and silent style of the past.

There is a gamut of possibilities between attempted absolute 'non-disclosure' by the analyst and mutual confession by both participants. But the *asymmetrical situation* is important, indeed I would argue key, to analysis—an essential means for exploring the transference: the analyst needs to remain, to a degree, an opaque (if not blank) 'screen' on to whom the patient's own unconscious feelings are transferred.

Patients may well be interested to examine the qualities in the clinician upon whom they have, after all, risked a good deal themselves. And often, of course, they do intuit real strength, weaknesses, or private beliefs in their analysts. Nonetheless, with the analyst deliberately holding back patients still make assumptions and assume answers, thereby giving indications about what they expect of themselves and of others. Too much actual information, in this sense, can be an unhelpful thing. This abstinence then enables the patient safely to picture the analyst as they please, and offers a better prospect of exploring the transference. That is why you cannot effectively and safely psychoanalyse a close friend or relative—they know too much of you, and you are too involved in their life.

Chapter 8
Unconscious dramas

Transference

Technique in analysis has increasingly been modelled around the recognition and exploration of transference; hence many analysts now would seek, as a matter of course, to make direct observations about the patient's unconscious attitudes towards them, even as the session proceeds. Much has also been written on how patients unconsciously 'nudge' their analysts to fit in with required roles, and how the clinician might stand in for someone else. Freud opened up this path, recognizing, for instance, that when patients seemed to fall in love with him a powerful emotion was actually transferred *on to him* from elsewhere.

This idea of transference can, admittedly, be used too formulaically and reduced to mantra, so that every interpretation becomes a banal attempt to show the patient, when talking of others, that it is *really* the analyst they have in mind, or conversely that when they address the analyst in a mood of affection, hate, or grievance they are in fact unconsciously relating to someone else.

There is also a risk of abusing the transference, just as there is in medical practice or an educational setting. Some clinicians, unfortunately, have taken advantage, exploiting patients' vulnerabilities to being bullied, seduced, or commanded by a charismatic figure. (A sad and troubling case that came to light of a talented and substantial contributor going off the rails was Masud Khan, a senior member of the British Psychoanalytical Society. His increasingly erratic behaviour with patients and colleagues ultimately proved impossible to ignore. The scale of his meltdown was to become a *cause célèbre* when exposed after his death by a former patient, Wynne Godley, in 2001.)

Freud had seen more than enough 'acting out' by colleagues, and he was alert to how unconscious factors were at work in their behaviour, as well as in the patient's. Indeed, the fact that powerful unconscious forces exist in all of us, and at times can break through to undermine the work, even shatter proceedings, was exactly what Freud's theories had anticipated and what analysis, supervision, the presentation of work at clinical seminars, and so on are designed as far as possible to contain.

Freud's own realization of the power of transference had first been brought home acutely with 'Dora', around the same time that *The Interpretation of Dreams* appeared. Dora had experienced him in much the same way, he concluded, that she had responded to another man, Herr K, with whom she had close family connections. Herr K had made a pass at her; she felt him to be indecent and intrusive, and pushed him away. How far Dora had secretly desired Herr K is another question. Some feminist commentators have built on Freud's own later recognition that her desire might have been for Herr K's wife (a possibility he had not sufficiently taken into account at the time of treatment). Herr K's interest was especially troubling to Dora because her father was apparently having an affair with Frau K. Dora suspected that her father was putting her in Herr K's way to distract and compensate him for the affair. Dora reacted extremely negatively when she felt pushed by Freud. The respective actions of Herr K and Freud in the case of Dora were not the same—her analyst was not seducing her—but the pressure she experienced in her treatment evoked in her a similarly claustrophobic and indignant reaction.

Initially, Freud had tended to think of transference as a nuisance, an unwarranted interference to overcome so that analyst and patient could continue to work unencumbered on, say, a dream. Yet he came to realize that understanding the transference was key to the work itself, or at least another important route into the study of the unconscious.

Counter-transference and enactment

Later on some analysts, especially in Britain, came to consider more fully the *counter-transference*, meaning the feelings or even behaviour unconsciously induced or amplified in an analyst by a particular patient. Some of those who developed the idea were colleagues of Klein, who in effect challenged her to rethink. Klein seemed sceptical about the value of the concept, fearing it risked self-indulgence, as Freud would probably have agreed.

Evidently the analyst also has his or her own transference to the patient (confusingly this is also sometimes referred to, more loosely, as counter-transference); but in addition to that, what always requires consideration, advocates of this approach now argued, is the unconscious response or feeling that may be prompted in the clinician by something in the patient's own character, style, and inner world.

'Go and have some more analysis!' So Paula Heimann (author of a seminal paper on counter-transference in 1950) was apparently advised when she suggested that she was powerfully affected by irrational feelings with certain patients. But Heimann's contribution proved lasting: analysts do indeed find such phenomena in themselves an important compass, a way of understanding what particular patients may evoke in, or project on to, them.

The problem for the analyst here is to acknowledge, differentiate, and make use of their feelings and experiences, and to try and sift out what belongs to whom. In a 1985 paper, 'Working Through in

the Countertransference', the analyst Irma Brenman Pick
described situations where a patient caused her to lose balance,
touching off acute feelings or inducing particular anxieties. Thus
one patient arrived, clearly unwell, saying 'I was determined to
come, even if that risks you getting my illness'. The analyst was
thereby agitated and felt vulnerable to his 'infection'; perhaps this
very feeling of helplessness was part of what the patient was
seeking to stir up. On another occasion she found herself feeling
rather flattered by the patient who commented effusively about
how well she had managed a public meeting at which he had been
present. Immediately thereafter he expressed 'concern' that he had
seen her smoking. She noticed her own immediate 'up and down'
mood, upon that combined message—the praise and then the
solicitous 'concern' and implicit criticism. These mood swings
were congruent with the patient's own oscillations, and that 'fit'
could be part of what the patient concerned may have
aimed at inducing.

Another very ill person, whose analysis continued during her time
in mental hospital, would turn up at the precise moment of the
end of the appointment, leaving the analyst feeling maddened and
despairing. On another occasion that patient arrived dishevelled,
with a powerful bodily odour, apparently quite without conscious
awareness of the impact of this. A key aspect of the task for the
analyst is to process these feelings as best she can. And the
patient, meanwhile, may well be monitoring, consciously or
unconsciously, how the analyst is struggling to deal with emotions
too—for instance defensively, omnipotently, honestly, or painfully.

It is always open to question how far the analyst's passing moods
in the consulting room are of a patient's making, so the idea of
counter-transference requires sensitive handling to ensure it is not
just a catch-all. Yet patients can be very skilful at touching off
sensitive areas in the analyst without appearing to do so. Perhaps
a patient is subtly winning over or needling in a way that leads the
practitioner to feel or to act in, say, an emollient, triumphant, or

angry fashion, even though unaware of this at the time. On other occasions it may be the apparent absence of feelings or a mood of complacency that is striking. In other words, the clinician, alert to this model, *tries* to take heed of what is more extreme than usual, or perhaps a manner of talking that is not really 'being herself', and then considers how it may be relevant.

A further term, 'enactment' or somewhat similarly 'actualization', is used to describe those moments when something is unconsciously happening *between* the participants. Enactment connotes the process where an analyst and patient seem to be caught up in a particular scene that expresses a phantasy, albeit played out between both parties. Enactments where analyst and patient waltz off together into some seriously inappropriate set of actions (commonly known as 'boundary violations') are ruinous to the analysis. Often, however, more subtle versions can become food for thought, retrievable and open to exploration within the treatment.

A patient crippled by a severe superego might find some pleasure in cruelty for instance, enjoying a certain 'sacrificial' position with sadistic sexual partners, and then produce echoes of this pattern in the analysis. This tendency may become apparent in a scenario where an analyst, normally restrained, finds herself almost 'haranguing' her patient, only to hear the latter breathe a contented sigh. We might suspect that something here has been played out that reflects the patient's unconscious, masochistic script. Such enactments can then be 'caught', and perhaps understood, potentially becoming an important vehicle for psychic change.

Finally, consider this moment in the treatment of a young woman who recalls to her male analyst a dream of herself at a dance. This account was published in a book by the analyst in question (Peter Giovacchini) and was further considered by another, Priscilla Roth. It is worth dwelling upon it now as a coda to this discussion of transference, counter-transference, and enactment.

The patient reports a hazy dream featuring a grey-suited man who asked her to dance. She adds how they moved around the room, whereupon her partner steered her to a corner and pressed himself against her. She could feel his erect penis. The analyst, in writing about the case, adds his own thoughts for the reader's benefit, observing that he often wore grey suits and the transference was erotic—the material providing an allusion 'to her sexual feeling toward me'.

The patient struggles, he notes, to defend herself against these impulses. He asks her to associate to the dream and then observes that she largely ignores this invitation, inclined to pursue other topics. She only hesitantly considers some elements in response to his prompt, such as the dream's obscurity. Her analyst then directs her back to the grey-suited man. Silent for a minute, the patient then becomes extremely anxious, reporting a sense of fogginess and the couch spinning. Gradually these feelings subside and she continues to talk but makes no reference to the dream.

Here the analyst becomes 'immensely curious', interrupts her and asks about the dream. To which she answers: 'What dream?' To his astonishment she has forgotten it. He repeats the details, brings her attention back to the man; once more she feels the couch turn furiously and seems to have wiped the dream from her memory. This 'dance' around the dream continues, with him even attempting a third pursuit of her associations, with the same results. As she experiences spinning sensations once more, she describes a vortex sucking in her thoughts.

We might well want to consider not only a patient's dream, in the manner that Freud did, but also what the patient is *doing* with the dream—in this case handing it over to her analyst and then apparently forgetting all about it. Moreover, given that analysts are well known to be particularly interested in such things, might it be that a particular patient, anxious to please or to repair things after a stormy session, might offer a dream as a kind of gift or peace offering, or even seductive gesture? Might it be used at times to provide analyst and patient with a mutually satisfying project, perhaps distracting them from something else? Thus one could approach in umpteen ways the function and manner of the telling of a dream, or of working on it in a session, alongside the specific issue of its contents and the associations that follow.

Levels of interpretation

Commenting on Giovacchini's report, Roth points to four levels of interpretation that might be made of the particular sequence just described. Most immediately (the first level), all of this could relate to the patient's father; perhaps he is the 'grey-suited' figure, by which one must include crucially not just the actual father, but the paternal figure that she has in mind. No doubt other material would inform such an assumption too, but let us assume 'grey suit' captures something of her father. Roth makes a link to Freud's Dora case, and how that patient experienced her father and Herr K in their dealings with her. The analyst could then have said to this young woman, as perhaps Freud might have done to Dora, 'Your dream is about your father; you are afraid to know you have these thoughts about your father'. One might also perhaps explore here the thoughts she believes her father has about her.

At a second level, an interpretation might focus directly upon the analyst: 'you are afraid of your dream because your dream is about me'. As Roth puts it, 'What [Giovacchini] shows us is an analyst in a session, trying to talk to his patient... about thoughts she had about him in the middle of the night called a dream.' The analyst has observed all of this to himself already, so could say: 'I often wear grey suits, the man in the dream wore a grey suit—in the middle of the night you had this fantasy about me.' This would be an interpretation about the transference of specific qualities, presented in a discrete fashion, and dealt with by the analyst from some distance.

At still another level, the analyst might ask what is happening *here and now*, and perhaps could say to the patient: 'There is something going on in this session in which I, interpreting to you, am being perceived as the man in the dream. It is as if the dream were repeating itself here.' So now the woman *in the session*, the woman who is *having the dream* and the woman *in the dream* are brought together as one. This interpretation could enable the analyst and patient to grasp how the same configuration has emerged in the session as in the dream.

Yet there is a fourth level too, where, as Roth puts it:

> we might consider the ways in which some combination of the patient's pressure and the difficulties this stirs up in the analyst lead to an unconsidered response by the analyst, to create the very situation at stake: an internal relationship is *in fact* being enacted within the session, an enactment in which both analyst and patient are taking part.

Some awareness of the possibility that this fourth level is in play could cause the analyst to reflect internally before speaking at all. This self-questioning about his counter-transference might then enable him to ask himself: 'Why do I find myself repeatedly pushing the patient into a corner? Why am I pressing my question on her?' The analyst here would first try to gain some kind of purchase upon this process before addressing the patient. Having done so he might be better able to consider how to make an interpretation without simply re-enacting the very process of 'pressing', as he is speaking. The analyst, in other words, could thereby think aloud with this patient and observe what keeps happening between them. In Roth's words: 'we seem to have arrived at a situation in which I am repeatedly pursuing you, or pushing you into a corner in a way that frightens you, as in your dream'.

Chapter 9
The struggle is not yet over

> I started my professional activity as a neurologist trying to
> bring relief to my neurotic patients. I discovered some
> important new facts about the unconscious...[and] the role
> of instinctual urges. Out of these findings grew a new science,
> psychoanalysis, a part of psychology, and a new method of
> treatment of the neuroses. I had to pay heavily for this bit of
> good luck. People did not believe in my facts and thought my
> theories unsavoury. Resistance was strong and unrelenting. In
> the end I succeeded...But the struggle is not yet over.

So Freud told the BBC in 1938. In the same breath he suggested
and undermined the notion that the status of psychoanalysis was
settled. Did Freud succeed 'in the end' as he hoped and claimed?
There will never be consensus, but in my view, in several senses,
the answer is yes. I want to conclude with a few further thoughts,
prompted by Freud's radio interview, regarding the achievements,
difficulties, impact, controversy, and possible political relevance of
the analytic approach.

Freud created an important field; produced a remarkable body of
writings; inspired innovations in culture, social theory, approaches
to biography, and political thought; built up a flourishing if often
fractious movement; encouraged many to follow in his tracks; and
established astonishing new paths of clinical and theoretical inquiry.

Analysis was from the start applied both directly to patients and to social phenomena, offering new perspectives on culture and collective beliefs. Some analysts admittedly became incautious, for instance conflating minds, groups, and nations, or treating characters in novels and plays as though patients on the couch, with little attention to the genre or context of the works in question.

We can argue this the other way too, noticing how Freud's real cases are artfully constructed, drawing on his great skills as a writer. He was steeped in the classics and his clinical accounts can be read as gripping stories. Many of Freud's theories resonate with ancient myths and the stories and theatrical dramas that he held most dear. But the dramatic quality also owes much, no doubt, to the manner in which the patients concerned recounted their troubles, how they too shaped the messiness of life into compelling narratives, revisiting and reworking their own histories.

Freud's BBC interview reminds us too that the dissemination of analysis is not confined to treatment behind closed doors, nor is it just the stuff of learned papers in professional societies: it is on the airwaves, in film, and now part of an ongoing conversation on Twitter, Facebook, and the rest. Elements of analysis passed into common language, as when people talk of themselves or others as being 'in denial' or 'repressed'.

Analysis is both an intensely private encounter and a public conversation that has by now gone on for more than a hundred years. Many cases have been published and it is also possible to read the reminiscences of, or interviews with, former patients which offer their own windows on to analytic experiences. These contain their share of acute observations and painful revelations, appreciation and praise, disappointment and humorous anecdote. Among the most evocative is the American poet and novelist Hilda Doolittle's *Tribute to Freud*, a record of her sessions in

Vienna during the 1930s. She found the talking cure haunting, poignant, revealing, and a dramatically life changing experience.

Sometimes an ambivalent, quizzical stance towards analysis has been used to powerful literary effect. Freud's writings were taken up admiringly, and also parodied by writers such as D. H. Lawrence. Among his engagements were appreciative but also wittily mocking essays on Freud's unconscious after World War I. Virginia Woolf, whose brother became an analyst, read Freud avidly late in her life and her diaries are seasoned with a few glowing impressions and more scathing asides about analysts she met and observed at close quarters. Freud's love of jokes and interest in puns were deftly trumped by James Joyce's artful references to his methods. There was an added poignancy to the allusions too, given that Joyce's daughter suffered serious mental illness. He wrote in *Finnegans Wake* of 'we grisly old Sykos', and a time when people 'were yung and easily freudened'.

'Now vee may perhaps to begin' is perhaps the most widely known psychoanalytical line of all in American fiction. Thus did the hitherto silent Dr Spielvogel (author of a solemn essay on 'The Puzzled Penis') conclude Philip Roth's *Portnoy's Complaint*, one of several notable post-war novels that take readers into the consulting room.

Images of analysts and patients in comedy and cartoons, especially in New York (and *The New Yorker*), or on television series (think of *The Sopranos* or *In Treatment*) would merit a book in their own right, as would the jokes that have featured in psychoanalytic writings or been directed back at the talking cure. Two will have to suffice: in the first, savoured by Freud, there is a married couple, one of whom says to the other: 'When one of us dies, I shall move to Paris'; in the second, following the death of his analyst a patient remarks to a friend: 'I would have gone to the funeral but he would have charged me for the session'.

Countless films revel in allusions to Freud, use the toolkit of analytic concepts, and/or satirize claims about the efficacy of the talking cure. Hitchcock's *Spellbound* (1945), with its dreamscapes by Salvador Dali, set the stage for the post-war Hollywood love affair with Freudian thought. Consider in turn how Žižek reinterprets and affectionately sends up the Freudian Hitchcock in his popular film *A Pervert's Guide to Cinema*. He places himself back on the water in the opening of *The Birds*, and even suggests that the layout of *Psycho* may be understood as a vision of the three-part Freudian mind. On the first floor, the ferocious (dead) mother—no father in sight—berating Norman Bates: this is the superego; on the ground floor, the reception area, where inner and outer worlds meet: the ego; in the basement, a terrifying cauldron of surprises: the id.

'Resistance was strong and unrelenting.' In a provocative argumentative manoeuvre some analysts, including Freud, have suggested that much public criticism (philosophical, literary, historical, religious, or scientific) could be discounted as merely the protestors' 'defensive' strategies against discomforting psychoanalytic insight. There may often enough be elements of truth in such 'diagnosis': Freud himself had indeed sometimes encountered knee-jerk resistance when he first set out his ideas, but according to analytic theory itself we are all bound, to some degree, to resist. This diagnostic approach to cultural critiques of analysis has led—understandably—to all the greater complaint: as though it might suffice for the analyst to interpret hostile motives, and be spared the bother of the critique itself. Some even turned the tables, suggesting here the analyst was defensively in search of bulletproof cover for his own assumptions and unargued beliefs.

If some criticisms of Freudian ideas or the analytical movement may be moralistic, crass, even hysterical, others are more troublesome to practitioners; certainly not all can be loftily dismissed as just 'defensive'. Among the most interesting challenges are some observational studies by social scientists that have described the internal workings of analytic groups and societies.

Ernest Gellner's mordant exploration of the profession is among the most famous. These inquiries have noted the degree to which the Freudian institutions acquired features of orthodoxy, redolent of religion, even as they analysed as illusory such tendencies elsewhere. A number of Freud's writings, such as *Totem and Taboo*, *Group Psychology*, and *Moses and Monotheism*, can also be seen as, among other things, oblique commentaries on the psychodynamics of the analytic movement itself.

It will always perhaps remain a contentious matter how far analysis should remain spontaneous, free, even 'romantic', in its creative aspiration; and to what degree codified, regimented, firm about technique and training, and insistent upon policing its boundaries. Many critics noted the irony when analysts, so probing in their accounts of the unconscious craving for authority, created requirements in their own organizations of rigid hierarchy and sometimes blinkered allegiance. One prominent analyst in America has referred to some current rigidities over training and other matters as akin to an institutional 'suicide note'. The analytic communities, various observers point out, are never short of rituals and devotional practices. The psychiatrist and writer Robert Jay Lifton, in a 1961 book on political 'thought reform' in Mao's China, touched in passing on an analytic institution in which he had started clinical training. He referred pointedly to 'milieu control', 'the supremacy of doctrine over experience', and 'sacred language'.

Looking to Britain, I'd argue that analysis benefited in several ways from its relative autonomy from other institutions, its independence from the medical profession, and its separation, for the most part, from the universities. But this very freedom of manoeuvre risked insulating and marginalizing the analytic community too. Sometimes analytic edicts were strikingly rigid, as when, in the 1930s, candidates were told they had to choose between working at the more publicly orientated and methodologically eclectic Tavistock Clinic in London and pursuing the more rarefied 'pure' analytic tradition championed by the British

Psychoanalytical Society (a requirement that Bion, among others, then notably defied).

In fact, many practitioners have managed to work effectively in dual settings, for instance in public health facilities or university departments. Thereby they could debate their claims with colleagues who use other methods of inquiry and of treatment; in this way analytic work could be disseminated *and* be made more open to revisions and critique from outside.

Analytic ideas about anxiety, defensiveness, denial, and enactment have value in the exploration of analytic institutions, and in probing the structure and unconscious interactions that occur within other professions too. Analysts have undertaken important studies for example of the often difficult emotional experiences of nurses, and investigated the ways they may find themselves routinely treated by doctors and managers in health services. They have also looked at what can go right—and wrong—in the practices of policing and of social work.

Not only in the 'caring professions', but also in industry, business, and the sciences, analysis has played a part in exploring the factors that facilitate creative, thoughtful work, or that destroy cohesion, that enable reality testing or delusional beliefs, that lead a group to spot dangers and intervene to deal with a crisis, become excessively alarmist, or, worse still, turn an insistently blind eye to the most harrowing human suffering.

The child psychotherapist Margaret Rustin well describes psychological, political, and interpersonal factors that led many professionals to fail to act upon evidence of the mortal dangers facing an eight-year-old child Victoria Climbié before she was murdered by her guardians in London in 2000, despite coming to the attention of the authorities many times. The case had attracted wide notice and precipitated a public inquiry. Rustin drew upon psychoanalytic ideas to show how and why it was possible for so many participant observers (doctors, social workers, teachers, police) in effect to refuse to see this horror, as is the case in many other comparable unfolding tragedies.

'Important new facts...a new science.' Freud certainly viewed and wanted it thus. To find himself exchanging letters in 1932 with Einstein on the subject of war and psychology, or six years later honoured by august scientists from the Royal Society, was for him far more important than avant-garde enthusiasm for his *Interpretation of Dreams*. Freud sought recognition, but tended to be unimpressed by the popular exploitation of analytic ideas, already so evident in interwar Europe.

One can only wonder what Freud would have made of a post-war buzzword such as 'shrink'; it is hard to believe he would have accepted it without interpreting the animus and fear it contains. An invitation Freud received in 1925 to collaborate on an American-financed film about Antony and Cleopatra left him cold, despite large promises of cash. He was equally underwhelmed when courted by artists such as Dali. Some of his colleagues however, including Karl Abraham, collaborated on films such as the silent German drama *Secrets of the Soul* (1926) directed by Georg Wilhelm Pabst.

With the spread of analytic ideas and societies came new rounds of criticism. Some attacked the talking cure for being unscientific, or worse a pseudo-science; for sapping the will, encouraging moral turpitude, or again for fostering rather than exploring and challenging narcissism. Freud had always made claims for analysis as a science, and this has laid it open to frequent attack. A caricature has it that the session is necessarily a catch-22 world, in which objection or disagreement by the patient is interpreted by rote as a defence against the truth of the analyst's certain interpretation.

The most influential version of the 'heads I win, tails you lose' critique came from the philosopher Karl Popper: although he admired Freud in part, he also argued that psychoanalysis was not scientific because it could never be 'falsified'. Scientific experiment, he claimed, presupposed the possibility of another scientist devising a means of showing that the first's hypothesis was not right.

Too often however, worst cases of analytic theorizing or practice come to be taken as the norm. Coercive or circular forms of persuasion—in writing, teaching, and in the consulting room—are certainly possible, but not in my experience necessary, still less inevitable, outcomes. Analysts with appropriate integrity are open to alternatives, seeking to remain aware they may not have understood, or to consider whether the treatment is helpful; their interpretations are best regarded as openings to investigation, not the last word. Even if the analyst interprets accurately, there is the further question about whether the timing is useful and bearable to the patient at that moment.

Debates about whether analysis is a science or not may also largely miss the point: its multiple contributions, clinically and culturally, need not ultimately hinge upon such verdicts either way. But before dismissing analysis as necessarily an unscientific procedure, you would need to ask yourself what alternative, more rigorous method might serve as well as this, in order to explore subjective experience and unconscious processes of the kind described in these pages. For at stake here is not the kind of knowledge you can glean from a brain scan, a treatise on philosophical logic, or questionnaire. Perhaps analysis needs to remain on the cusp, *aiming* at rigour, open to the complication, even falsification, of its own truth claims, while concerned above all with creativity and effectiveness along the lines of an experimental craft or art.

Idealization of analysis is as possible as demonization, and can also be damaging. As the ever more popular Pope Francis quipped in 2014 in response to the phenomenon of 'Francescomania': 'Sigmund Freud used to say...that in every idealisation there is an attack' (as quoted in the *Guardian*, 6 March 2014). He may well be the first leader of the Catholic Church to make use of Freud so directly in an interpretation of the excesses of devotion to a man, or a cause, and the possible aggression behind it. Ambivalence, according to Freud, is likely to be aroused in all of us by analysis itself, and those who profess *only* their undying love of the talking cure would of course also be suitable cases for its treatment.

Freud's desire was to shake up the way we habitually think, hear, and see, and to insist on treating phantasy and dreams as central to our lives. He was also ever determined in his attempts to seek psychic roots, and provide new routes to the study of the unconscious. His cases, it has been said, had certain affinities with the genre of detective stories, which also came of age in the late Victorian period when analysis was invented. Some have likened Freud to a Sherlock Holmes, connoisseur of overlooked clues. Freud also compared himself to a *conquistador*.

But as the original circle of devotees expanded, and analysis developed into a more formal empire of knowledge, something of the early, buccaneering spirit was lost. Like other professional organizations of worldwide scale, psychoanalytic institutions inevitably and in many ways necessarily tightened up as they moved from an early exploratory phase to a more settled stage of development. Very few clinicians within the field, admittedly, have even a trace of Freud's genius for *writing*, and none have matched the boldness of his experiments in both thought and practice. Nonetheless the field continues to evolve, open to innovation and development, not only in the consulting room but also in its other applications, such as therapeutic work in schools or with families and groups. Analysis is, in short, a continuing work in progress.

'Experience has taught us that psycho-analytic therapy—the liberation of a human being from his neurotic symptoms, inhibitions and abnormalities of character—is a lengthy business', Freud remarked in 1937 in one of his final essays, 'Analysis Terminable and Interminable'. Part of the problem was indeed the time the work takes. Freud celebrated what analysis made possible, but also seemed troubled by the puzzle of why deeper psychic change can be so slow moving, and how in some cases symptoms or other serious life difficulties returned to afflict previously treated patients. There may well be a constant struggle, as recent analysts have suggested, between the desire for psychic equilibrium and for change.

Typical analyses grew longer in the course of the 20th century. Now, however, the reverse may be happening. The time-consuming form of classical analysis has placed it on a collision course with the ever more hectic circumstances, and the predominant values of speed in our contemporary age. We live in a culture and economy that assumes, clamorously, the case for endless 'growth', and that measures its 'results' on the narrowest of terms and with the shortest of timescales. True, there is much to be said for administrative efficiency, and, not least in the health service, for minimizing waiting lists or auditing the successes and failures of professional service providers. Pressure to reduce delay and test cost effectiveness has become, understandably, ever greater in these financially straitened times. But speed of delivery has also become for many an unquestioned value in itself. The Internet no doubt feeds into this, encouraging us to expect an instant response to *any* of our questions, with demand met by supply in split seconds.

Many service users even in relatively well-organized health systems such as Britain's, report their impressions that less and less regard is paid to the human experience and quality of care, with insufficient time allowed to provide much by way of human contact. A culture of 'targets' has too often neglected the psychological element—for example the importance, where possible, of seeing the same person continuously over time, not just being assigned an interchangeable, anonymous doctor. Bed-ridden patients may benefit too from a few minutes talking with a nurse, who is not simply undertaking a designated function and speeding past 'efficiently'. (This tendency is apparent in many other fields too: note how school children's and their teachers' time is ever more accounted for, in the UK at least, with what often seem deadening and endless tests.) Supposedly 'slack' time out of which new ideas can emerge may now be dismissed as unaffordable, a luxury, or the preserve of 'losers'.

Some critics of analytic psychotherapy, including various prominent gurus of modern 'happiness', suggest that a short course of CBT suffices anyway to get the show back on the road, and insist that the longer-term therapies, and the entire notion of the Freudian unconscious, can be consigned to the dustbin of history. Clearly in most public health facilities it is highly unlikely that the classical, open-ended approach that Freud pioneered will ever be possible when resources are so scarce. But analysis seems to be reviled and at risk of being removed even from the small spaces it had previously occupied within health services, precisely because it may invite us to question the very framework within which we are operating.

Certainly analysis requires that we pause and allow space for second, or third, thoughts. And in its basic ethos perhaps it stands out too against a culture that values human inquiry, education, or social investment only by the next quarterly profit figures. Moreover, it offers a way to think about the defences that exist against facing the mutual dependency that is a fact of life for all of us. To contrast with Bion's psychotic clockwork man, whom I described in Chapter 7, it might be worth recalling Herbert Marcuse's vision of a more pervasive and ordinary modern impoverishment, captured in a book he entitled *One Dimensional Man*.

Meanwhile, in recent decades various scholars have devoted great energy to the compilation of 'black books' on all that has gone awry within the analytic profession since Freud invented the procedure. The list is certainly not short. But the question of the continuing relevance of psychoanalysis is far from a settled argument. Even within contemporary neuroscience, there is a resurgence of interest in and support for Freud's models of the mind, a renewed wish by some to marry the disciplines, thereby belatedly fulfilling Freud's own desire that these fields would one day converge. But one might also argue that there should be no cause for lament if analysis retains its particular edge and focus, without too anxiously seeking to amalgamate itself with other modes of thought or science.

There is no space here to delve further into such loaded terms as 'outcomes', 'happiness', 'fulfilment', or 'improvement', let alone 'cure'. Of course there is some value in seeking to test therapeutic methods, so that a patient with bipolar symptoms, an eating disorder, an obsessional compulsion, or acute depression is appropriately referred for treatment to this specialism or that. Yet we must also recognize that clustering patients into groups, defined by symptoms, might easily draw us back towards the terrain of an old psychiatry, and its questionable classificatory schemas where people tend no longer to be viewed in their complex individuality.

In fact a lively debate is in progress, and trials, and scrutiny, of 'outcomes' are now in full swing. CBT is by far the most widely tested method (in part because its advocates have for decades tended to be enthusiasts of such empirical testing in the first place). And as a recent study *What Works for Whom?* warns: 'In the worst case, we could arrive at a monoculture in which CBT became eponymous with evidence-based practice.'

We would need to ponder further the question of what analysis is best served to do, before instantly giving an answer to how it might be 'tested'. A movement of 'anti-psychiatrists' led by R. D. Laing pointed out over fifty years ago that to measure the success of a method by its capacity to adjust the putatively mentally ill to a 'mad' realm outside, in the polity, or in the family, begged the very questions that most urgently needed asking. While I would argue, unlike some of those anti-psychiatrists at their most combative, that there is indeed such a thing as mental illness, I would endorse their view that neither analytic work, nor for that matter psychiatry, nor any other form of therapy, should be there to manufacture conformity or, like some World War I shellshock doctors, regard cure to mean simply the presumed fitness of the patient to return to active service in the trenches.

Well may we lament in our own time the facile and pernicious reduction of the human being to *Homo economicus*, and rail against the short-termism of most dominant contemporary forms of political thought. Psychoanalysis has long been an important part of the toolkit in the study of political ideology; it may be as potentially useful in considering denials of greed and aggression in utopian communism as the murderous paths of fundamentalist, fascist, or totalitarian fervour; and it may also help illuminate the complacent occlusions of reality that are required in states of liberal cynicism or self-congratulatory capitalism as well.

To understand how politics and psyches interact, we cannot bypass the realm of phantasy and the role of defences. Of course, particular and powerful material interests knowingly bend truth, for instance employing manipulative lobbyists to throw dust into our eyes, to foster avarice, or to justify cut-throat competition and a 'winner takes all' mentality. But a propensity to myopia and a tendency to wishful thinking are all too easily stirred up, because, as Freud showed, there is much we all may prefer, quite actively and insistently, not to know, even when the means of knowing are available. Manic and omnipotent states of mind can exist, analysis suggests, in all of us. One can see as vividly in the consulting room as in the political arena, for example, how awareness of vulnerability can be denied, or the capacity to protect and nurture a viable, liveable future mocked, dismissed, or trivialized.

A myriad of factors, to take a pressing example of global import, now converge to threaten environmental havoc. Many communities, even entire states, are in jeopardy, to say nothing of the threat of extinction for numerous other species across large areas of the planet as the climate continues to change. Psychoanalytic thought is no substitute for practical struggles for greater social justice or for a different economic settlement. Yet analysis has a valuable contribution to offer in examining how we may opt to avoid considering even the possibility of other ways of living, or facing square on, 'an inconvenient truth'.

Suffice to say here that analytic thought may yet have some role to play in such urgent political debates, and in challenging what passes, individually or collectively, for the given 'order of things'. Certainly psychoanalysis remains an important antidote to the current assumption that quick fixes, personal or political, are always good value. Perhaps the analytic method might even be compared to the return of the slow food movement in the age of the Big Mac.

Mournful or gleeful obituaries have existed almost as long as psychoanalysis. And I am far from the first to insist that these requiems to the talking cure should invite the same dry response as Mark Twain's: 'The report of my death was an exaggeration.'

A note on confidentiality

As noted in this text, the identity of some of Freud's patients and those of other early pioneers was later unmasked. The importance of confidentiality in clinical discussions and publications grew to become an ever more pressing ethical concern. Yet the communication of analytic knowledge requires detailed illustration to come alive.

Since no two cases are ever identical, it would be a gross impoverishment only to speak in generalities. Some clinicians opt routinely to ask patients' permission before drawing on any of their material; others criticize this tendency, pointing to how it interferes with analysis, and note how even a request after a treatment might be an unwarranted intrusion.

If one option would be to eschew publication, another is to combine features of several patients and use other forms of camouflage sufficient to protect identities. The point usually, in clinical writing, is to focus the reader's attention on a particular aspect of a case, without pretending to offer an elaborate portrait, in the manner, say, of Freud's own book-length studies of patients.

We may need to rely more in future upon the writings of ex-patients themselves, such as those eloquent autobiographical reflections described in Chapter 1. As is commonplace nowadays, clinical vignettes used in the present text, drawn from my own or colleagues' experiences, are heavily disguised.

Further reading

Readers wishing to deepen their knowledge will find the online resource PEPWEB invaluable, as it provides many major psychoanalytic journals, including the *International Journal of Psychoanalysis* (*IJP*), classic books, and helpful glossaries. It contains the *Standard Edition of the Complete Works of Freud* (*SE*), which is also available in print. Freud's writings can be read in several other paperback versions, for instance, in an older Pelican series, or the recent Penguin Modern Classics range. *The Freud Reader* (New York, 1989), edited by Peter Gay, offers a synthesis of key writings and a useful timeline.

Chapter 1: Introduction

David Bell, *Paranoia* (Duxford, 2003).

Josh Cohen, *The Private Life: Why We Remain in the Dark* (London, 2013).

Julia Fabricius, Jane Milton, and Caroline Polmear, *A Short Introduction to Psychoanalysis* (London, 2004).

Anna Freud, 'On the Theory of Analysis of Children', *IJP* (1929), vol. 10, pp. 29–38.

Sigmund Freud, 'The Case of Schreber' [1911], *SE*, Volume 12.

Sigmund Freud, 'An Autobiographical Study' [1925], *SE*, Volume 20.

Stephen Frosh, *Key Concepts in Psychoanalysis* (London, 2002).

Stephen Grosz, *The Examined Life: How We Lose and Find Ourselves* (London, 2013).

Melanie Klein, *Narrative of a Child Analysis: The Conduct of the Psycho-Analysis of Children as seen in the Treatment of a Ten Year Old Boy* (London, 1961).

Julia Kristeva, *Black Sun: Depression and Melancholia* (New York, 1989).

Darian Leader, *What Is Madness?* (London, 2011).

Jonathan Lear, *Freud* (London, 2005).

Joyce McDougal, *Theatres of the Mind: Illusion and Truth on the Psychoanalytic Stage* (London, 1985).

Elyn Saks, *The Center Cannot Hold: My Journey Through Madness* (New York, 2007).

Daniel Paul Schreber, *Memoirs of My Nervous Illness* (Cambridge, 1988).

Ella Freeman Sharpe, 'The Technique of Psycho-Analysis', *IJP* (1931), vol. 12, pp. 24–60.

Anthony Stevens, *Jung: A Very Short Introduction* (Oxford, 2001).

Anthony Storr, *Freud: A Very Short Introduction* (Oxford, 1989).

Barbara Taylor, *The Last Asylum: A Memoir of Madness in Our Times* (London, 2014).

Chapter 2: How psychoanalysis began

Josef Breuer and Sigmund Freud, *Studies on Hysteria* [1895], *SE*, Volume 2.

Sigmund Freud, *The Interpretation of Dreams* [1900], *SE*, Volumes 4 and 5.

Sigmund Freud, *The Psychopathology of Everyday Life* [1901], *SE*, Volume 6.

Sigmund Freud, *Three Essays on the Theory of Sexuality* [1905], *SE*, Volume 7.

Sigmund Freud, *Jokes and their Relation to the Unconscious* [1905], *SE*, Volume 5.

Sigmund Freud, 'Creative Writers and Day-Dreaming' [1908], *SE*, Volume 9.

Sigmund Freud, 'Formulations on the Two Principles of Mental Functioning' [1911], *SE*, Volume 12.

Jean Laplanche, 'The Kent Seminar, 1 May 1990', in John Fletcher and Martin Stanton (eds), *Jean Laplanche: Seduction, Translation and the Drives* (London, 1992), pp. 21–40.

Jean Laplanche and Jean-Bertrand Pontalis, *The Language of Psycho-Analysis* (London, 1973).

George Makari, *Revolution in Mind: The Creation of Psychoanalysis* (New York, 2008).

Daniel Pick and Lyndal Roper (eds), *Dreams and History: The Interpretation of Dreams from Ancient Greece to Modern Psychoanalysis* (Hove, 2004).

Karl Schorkse, *Fin-de-Siècle Vienna: Politics and Culture* (New York, 1961).

Richard Skues, *Sigmund Freud and the History of Anna O: Reopening a Closed Case* (London, 2006).

Frank J. Sulloway, *Freud, Biologist of the Mind: Beyond the Psychoanalytic Legend* (London, 1979).

Eli Zaretsky, *Secrets of the Soul: A Social and Cultural History of Psychoanalysis* (New York, 2004).

Chapter 3: A case of obsessional neurosis

Sigmund Freud, 'Notes Upon a Case of Obsessional Neurosis' [1909], *SE*, Volume 10.

Sigmund Freud, *The Ego and the Id* [1923], *SE*, Volume 19.

Patrick Mahony, *Freud and the Rat Man* (New Haven, 1986).

Edna O'Shaughnessy, 'Relating to the Superego', *IJP* (1999), vol. 80, pp. 861–70.

John Steiner, *Psychic Retreats: Pathological Organizations in Psychotic, Neurotic, and Borderline Patients* (London, 1993).

Chapter 4: Oedipus

Wilfred Bion, 'The Imaginary Twin', in *Second Thoughts: Selected Papers on Psychoanalysis* (London, 1967), pp. 3–22.

Ronald Britton, Michael Feldman, and Edna O'Shaughnessy, *The Oedipus Complex Today* (London, 1989).

Judith Butler, *Gender Trouble: Feminism and the Subversion of Identity* (London, 1990).

Gilles Deleuze and Felix Guattari, *Anti-Oedipus: Capitalism and Schizophrenia* [1972] (London, 1983).

Sigmund Freud, *From the History of an Infantile Neurosis (The 'Wolf Man')* [1918], *SE*, Volume 17.

Margaret Mahler, 'On the First Three Subphases of the Separation-Individuation Process', *IJP* (1972), vol. 53, pp. 333–8.

Juliet Mitchell, *Psychoanalysis and Feminism: A Radical Reassessment of Freudian Psychoanalysis* (London, 1974).

Juliet Mitchell, *Siblings: Sex and Violence* (Oxford, 2003).

Joan Riviere, 'Womanliness As a Masquerade', *IJP* (1929), vol. 10, pp. 303–13.

John Steiner, 'Turning a Blind Eye: The Cover up for Oedipus',
    International Review of Psycho-Analysis (1985), vol. 12,
    pp. 161–72. Also published in his *Psychic Retreats*.
Margot Waddell, *Inside Lives: Psychoanalysis and the Growth of the
    Personality*, revised edition (London, 2002).

Chapter 5: Analytic space, time, and technique

Jessica Benjamin, 'Beyond Doer and Done To: An Intersubjective
    View of Thirdness', *Psychoanalytical Quarterly* (2004), vol. 73,
    pp. 5–46.
Christopher Bollas and David Sundelson, *The New Informants:
    Betrayal of Confidentiality in Psychoanalysis and Psychotherapy*
    (London, 1995).
John Bowlby, *Attachment and Loss*, Volume 1 (London, 1969).
Franco De Masi, *Making Death Thinkable* (London, 2004).
Michael Feldman, *Doubt, Conviction and the Analytic Process:
    Selected Papers* (Hove, 2009).
Bruce Fink, *A Clinical Introduction to Lacanian Psychoanalysis:
    Theory and Technique* (London, 1997).
Peter Fonagy, 'The Changing Shape of Clinical Practice: Driven by
    Science or by Pragmatics?' *Psychoanalytic Psychotherapy* (2010),
    vol. 24, pp. 22–43.
John Forrester, 'Dead on Time: Lacan's Theory of Temporality', in *The
    Seductions of Psychoanalysis: Freud, Lacan and Derrida*
    (Cambridge, 1991), pp. 168–218.
Betty Joseph, *Psychic Equilibrium and Psychic Change: Selected
    Papers of Betty Joseph*, ed. Michael Feldman and Elizabeth Bott
    Spillius (London, 1989).
Jacques Lacan, *Écrits*, trans. Bruce Fink (London, 2006).
Herbert Rosenfeld, *Psychotic States: A Psychoanalytic Approach*
    (London, 1965).
Elisabeth Roudinesco, *Jacques Lacan and Co: A History of
    Psychoanalysis in France* (London, 1990).
Michael Rustin, 'The Generation of Psychoanalytic Knowledge:
    Sociological and Clinical Perspectives Part One: "Give Me a
    Consulting Room"', *British Journal of Psychotherapy* (1997),
    vol. 13, pp. 527–41.
Sherry Turkle, *Psychoanalytical Politics: Jacques Lacan and Freud's
    French Revolution* (London, 1992).

Chapter 6: War, politics, and ideas

Geoffrey Cocks, *Psychotherapy in the Third Reich: The Göring Institute* (Oxford, 1985).

Joy Damousi and Mariano Ben Plotkin (eds), *Psychoanalysis and Politics: Histories of Psychoanalysis Under Conditions of Restricted Political Freedom* (Oxford, 2012).

Matt ffytche, 'Freud and the Neocons: The Narrative of a Political Encounter from 1949–2000', *Psychoanalysis and History* (2013), vol. 15, pp. 5–44.

Sigmund Freud, *Beyond the Pleasure Principle* [1920], *SE*, Volume 18.

Sigmund Freud, 'Inhibitions, Symptoms and Anxiety' [1926], *SE*, Volume 20.

Sigmund Freud, *Civilization and Its Discontents* [1930], *SE*, Volume 21.

Erich Fromm, *The Anatomy of Human Destructiveness* (New York, 1973).

Stephen Frosh, *Hate and the 'Jewish Science': Anti-Semitism, Nazism and Psychoanalysis* (Basingstoke, 2009).

Nathan Hale, *The Rise and Crisis of Psychoanalysis in the United States, 1917–1985* (New York, 1995).

Tom Harrison, *Bion, Rickman, Foulkes, and the Northfield Experiments: Advancing on a Different Front* (London, 2000).

Martin Jay, *The Dialectical Imagination: A History of the Frankfurt School and the Institute of Social Research, 1923–1950* (London, 1996).

Walter Kendrick and Perry Meisel (eds), *Bloomsbury/Freud: The Letters of James and Alix Strachey, 1924–1925* (New York, 1985).

Pearl King and Riccardo Steiner (eds), *The Freud–Klein Controversies 1941–1945* (London, 1991).

Daniel Pick, *The Pursuit of the Nazi Mind: Hitler, Hess, and the Analysts* (Oxford, 2012).

Edward Said, *Freud and the Non-European*, with an introduction by Christopher Bollas and a response by Jacqueline Rose (London 2003).

Hanna Segal, *Psychoanalysis, Literature and War: Papers 1972–1995* (London, 1997).

Michal Shapira, *The War Inside: Psychoanalysis, Total War, and the Making of the Democratic Self in Postwar Britain* (Cambridge, 2013).

Chapter 7: Further innovations and controversies

Jan Abram, *The Language of Winnicott: A Dictionary and Guide to Understanding his Work* (London, 1996).

Robin Anderson (ed.), *Clinical Lectures on Klein and Bion* (London, 1992).

Wilfred Bion, *Second Thoughts: Selected Papers on Psycho-Analysis* (London, 1967).

Wilfred Bion, *The Long Week-End 1897–1919: Part of a Life* (London, 1982).

Dana Birksted-Breen, Sara Flanders, and Alain Gibeault (eds), *Reading French Psychoanalysis* (London, 2010).

Malcolm Bowie, *Lacan* (London, 1991).

Peter Fonagy, *Attachment Theory and Psychoanalysis* (New York, 2001).

Anna Freud, *The Ego and the Mechanisms of Defence* (London, 1937).

Sigmund Freud, 'Observations on Transference-Love (Further Recommendations on the Technique of Psycho-Analysis III)' [1915], in *SE*, Volume 12.

Heinz Hartmann, 'Psychoanalysis and the Concept of Health', *IJP* (1939), vol. 20, pp. 308–21.

Jeremy Holmes, *John Bowlby and Attachment Theory* (London, 1993).

Melanie Klein, *The Psychoanalysis of Children* [1932] (London, 1989).

Jacques Lacan, 'The Mirror-Stage As Formative of the I Function As Revealed in Psychoanalytic Experience', *Écrits*, trans. B. Fink (London, 2006), pp. 75–81.

Jean Laplanche, 'Jean Laplanche talks to Martin Stanton', *Free Associations* (1991), vol. 2, pp. 323–41.

Meira Likierman, *Melanie Klein: Her Work in Context* (London, 2001).

Stephen A. Mitchell (ed.) *Relationality: From Attachment to Intersubjectivity* (Hillsdale, 2000).

Denise Riley, *War in the Nursery: Theories of the Child and Mother* (London, 1983).

Roy Schafer, *Tradition and Change in Analysis* (London, 1997).

Hanna Segal, *Klein* (London, 1989).

Donald Winnicott, *The Child and the Family* (London, 1957).

Donald Winnicott, *The Maturational Processes and the Facilitating Environment: Studies in the Theory of Emotional Development* (London, 1965).

Slavoj Žižek, *Lacan* (London, 2006).

Chapter 8: Unconscious dramas

A. W. Bateman, 'Thick- and Thin-Skinned Organisations and Enactment in Borderline and Narcissistic Disorders', *IJP* (1998), vol. 79, pp. 13–26.

Irma Brenman Pick, 'Working Through in the Countertransference',
    IJP (1985), vol. 66, pp. 157–66.
Sigmund Freud, *Fragment of an Analysis of a Case of Hysteria (Dora)*
    [1905], *SE*, Volume 7.
Peter Giovacchini, *Clinician's Guide to Reading Freud* (New York,
    1982).
Wynne Godley, 'Saving Masud Khan', *London Review of Books*, 22
    February 2001, pp. 3–7.
Paula Heimann, 'On Counter-Transference', *IJP* (1950), vol. 31,
    pp. 81–4.
Priscilla Roth, 'Mapping the Landscape: Levels of Transference
    Interpretation', *IJP* (2001), vol. 82, pp. 1055–61.
Joseph Sandler, 'Actualization and Object Relationships', *Journal of
    Philadelphia Association for Psychoanalysis* (1977), vol. 4, pp. 59–70.

Chapter 9: The struggle is not yet over

Michael Balint, *The Doctor, His Patient, and the Illness* (Edinburgh, 1964).
Janet Bergstrom (ed.), *Endless Night: Cinema and Psychoanalysis,
    Parallel Histories* (London, 1999).
Malcolm Bowie, et al. (eds), *Modernism and the European
    Unconscious* (Cambridge, 1990).
Hilda Doolittle, *Tribute to Freud* (Oxford, 1971).
Sigmund Freud, 'Analysis Terminable and Interminable' [1937], in *SE*,
    Volume 23.
Stephen Frosh, *Psychoanalysis Outside the Clinic* (London, 2010).
Peter Gay, *Freud for Historians* (New York, 1985).
Ernest Gellner, *The Psychoanalytic Movement: Or the Coming of
    Unreason* (London, 1985).
Otto Kernberg, 'Suicide Prevention for Psychoanalytic Institutes and
    Societies', *Journal of the American Psychoanalytic Association*
    (2013), vol. 61, pp. 771–86.
D. H. Lawrence, *Psychoanalysis and the Unconscious* and *Fantasia of
    the Unconscious* [1923] (Cambridge, 2004).
Robert Jay Lifton, *Thought Reform and the Psychology of 'Totalism':
    A Study of 'Brainwashing' in China* (London, 1961).
Herbert Marcuse, *One-Dimensional Man: Studies in the Ideology of
    Advanced Industrial Society* (London, 1964).
Isabel Menzies-Lyth, 'Social Systems As a Defence against Anxiety'
    [1960], republished in *Containing Anxiety in Institutions*, Volume 1
    (London, 1988).

Karin Obholzer, *The Wolf-Man: Conversations with Freud's Patient—Sixty Years Later* (New York, 1982).

Karl Popper, *Conjectures and Refutations: The Growth of Scientific Knowledge* (London, 1963).

Jacqueline Rose, *States of Fantasy* (Oxford, 1996).

Anthony Roth and Peter Fonagy, *What Works for Whom? A Critical Review of Psychotherapy Research* (New York, 2005).

Elisabeth Roudinesco, *Lacan: In Spite of Everything* (London, 2014).

Margaret Rustin, 'Conceptual Analysis of Critical Moments in Victoria Climbié's Life', *Child and Family Social Work* (2005), vol. 10, pp. 11–19.

Sebastiano Timpanaro, *The Freudian Slip: Psychoanalysis and Textual Criticism* (London, 1976).

Sally Weintrobe, *Engaging with Climate Change: Psychoanalytic and Interdisciplinary Perspectives* (London, 2012).

Virginia Woolf, *The Diary of Virginia Woolf*, Volume 5, 1936–41 (London 1984).

Slavoj Žižek, *The Pervert's Guide to Cinema*, DVD (2007).

Index

SOCIAL MEDIA
Very Short Introduction

Join our community
www.oup.com/vsi

- Join us online at the official Very Short Introductions **Facebook** page.
- Access the thoughts and musings of our authors with our online **blog**.
- Sign up for our monthly **e-newsletter** to receive information on all new titles publishing that month.
- Browse the full range of Very Short Introductions online.
- Read **extracts** from the Introductions for free.
- Visit our library of **Reading Guides**. These guides, written by our expert authors will help you to question again, why you think what you think.
- If you are a teacher or lecturer you can order inspection copies quickly and simply via our website.